The Craft of Dying

The Craft of Dying

The Modern Face of Death
40th Anniversary Edition

Lyn H. Lofland
Introduction by John Troyer
Epilogue by Ara A. Francis

The MIT Press
Cambridge, Massachusetts
London, England

This book was set in ITC Stone Serif Std and ITC Stone Sans Std by Toppan Best-set Premedia Limited. Printed and bound in the United States of America.

Library of Congress Cataloging-in-Publication Data

Names: Lofland, Lyn H., author.
Title: The craft of dying : the modern face of death / Lyn H. Lofland ; introduction by John Troyer ; epilogue by Ara A. Francis.
Description: 40th anniversary edition. | Cambridge, MA : The MIT Press, [2019] | Originally published: Beverly Hills : Sage Publications, 1978. | Includes bibliographical references and index.
Identifiers: LCCN 2018046339 | ISBN 9780262537346 (pbk. : alk. paper)
Subjects: LCSH: Death--Psychological aspects. | Death--Social aspects.
Classification: LCC BF789.D4 L63 2019 | DDC 155.9/37--dc23 LC record available at https://lccn.loc.gov/2018046339

10 9 8 7 6 5 4 3 2 1

For
Estelle Hogan Hebert
and
John F. Hogins, Jr.

Contents

Introduction

John Troyer

Lyn Lofland's *The Craft of Dying* (1978) is one of the most important books on post-WWII death and dying practices that almost no one has read. To see Lofland's largely overlooked, but still relevant, text republished by the MIT Press is both thrilling and deeply gratifying. It is the one book that in my capacity as Director of the Centre for Death and Society at the University of Bath I think every person working on contemporary death and dying issues must read. Indeed, I strongly recommend that anyone interested in understanding how events forty-years ago shaped what Lofland would call today's "thanatological chic" read *The Craft of Dying* and note the current uncanny resemblances to the 1970s.

The Craft of Dying is, for me, *that* death, dying, and end-of-life issues book.

A common response to my adamant recommendation is—why? Why and how is this specific book any different or better than its contemporaries, e.g., *On Death and Dying* by Elisabeth Kübler-Ross or *The Denial of Death* by Ernest Becker (to name two big death canon contenders)? My rapid answer is that Lofland's book both documents what happened in the 1970s (the formation of new hospice spaces, activist groups encouraging people to accept death, the introduction of college courses on dying, and so on) alongside an invaluable critique of those activities. In fact, it is Lofland's critique and classification of death-focused groups as *social movements* creatively constructing a new end-of-life ideology that makes *The Craft of Dying* fundamentally important. Lofland calls these end-of-life groups (similar in structure, she will note, to diffuse 1970s women's movement and environmental movement groups) the happy death movement and uses the term to connote enthusiastic warriors taking on a challenge (see part III, Collective Constructions: The Happy Death Movement). Her critique is both generous and insightful at all times. But Lofland was not content with merely documenting what these death and dying groups did; she wanted to better understand what motivated their new end-of-life politics and thinking. It is her push to clearly articulate what is happening in her own moment that makes *The Craft of Dying* so valuable today; almost every argument and observation she first presented forty years ago remain both pertinent and urgently needed now.

This book is truly a message in a bottle, and one sent from a decade when death and dying social movements coalesced around end-of-life ideologies that the Western world still struggles with today. That Lyn Lofland accomplished this feat in so few pages is an achievement in and of itself.

Discovering *The Craft of Dying*

For all my praise of Lofland's work, I am embarrassed to say that I first learned of, and then read, *The Craft of Dying* in summer 2014. My mid-career discovery of Lofland occurred only after my esteemed colleague (and walking Death Studies encyclopedia) Tony Walter asked if I knew her book and the happy death movement argument. I said that no, I didn't. Tony asked about Lofland, because he understood how *The Craft of Dying* directly related to my (then new) research project on American death and dying discourse during the 1970s.

In a nutshell, this research project examines how the 1970s functioned as a crucial but largely forgotten decade for understanding what motivates today's death and dying groups, as well as foreshadowing many current end-of-life debates. It is during the 1970s that new death and dying tools and technologies took root, altering the definition of death: things taken for granted today, such as living wills and life-support technologies. Much of the decade's activity is at a very local level and includes individuals forming groups that emphasize Death Acceptance, the Right-to-Die, and dying a Natural Death—all thoroughly documented in *The Craft of Dying*.

But the 1970s was also a decade when end-of-life issues extended all the way to the White House and bookended politically tumultuous times. In 1971 President Richard Nixon announced his War on Cancer, and in 1979 President Jimmy Carter formed the President's Commission for the Study of Ethical Problems in Medicine and Biomedical Behavioral Research, which later published its landmark 1981 report *Defining Death: A Report on the Medical, Legal, and Ethical Issues in the Determination of Death* during the Reagan administration. Carter's group would eventually become known as the President's Council on Bioethics and advise all future Presidents on a wide array of issues, including, but not limited to, death and dying.

Lofland's research remains a key historical and conceptual anchor for anyone interested in that decade, since *The Craft of Dying* analyzed and critiqued what was happening in the 1970s, *during the 1970s*. What any reader comes away with from this book, I think, is how death and dying were national conversations related to ongoing events—e.g., the Karen Ann Quinlan right-to-die case in New Jersey (which also went global)—and connected to personal freedoms—e.g., the country's first Natural Death Act, passed in California in 1976, that gave individuals the right to legally refuse medical treatments even if the refusal meant dying.

After Tony Walter's helpful nudge, I discovered that *The Craft of Dying* was long out of print (the republishing idea first occurred in this very moment), but I persisted in locating a copy and subsequently devoured the book in one August 2014 sitting. I say in all seriousness that reading this book fundamentally changed how I approached all research on death, dying, the dead body, end-of-life concerns, the politics of death, the historical formation of hospice spaces, current Happy Death groups pushing for what Lofland has called "death talk," and neoliberal economic "choice" about funerals. I could go on and on. And like any convert with a newly discovered evangelical zeal I wanted nothing more than to excitedly read long sections of *The Craft of Dying* to audiences.

Coincidentally enough, captive audiences were available to me in August 2014, since I was the Scholar in Residence at the Morbid Anatomy Museum in Brooklyn, New York (now sadly closed). I am not kidding when I say that almost all my public lectures during the residency involved me simply reading sections from *The Craft of Dying*, especially the introduction:

> It seems likely that eventually humans will construct for themselves a new, or at least altered, death culture and organization—a new "craft of dying"—better able to contain the new experience. I believe, as do other sociological observers ... that in the ferment of activity relative to death and dying during the last two decades in the United States

we have witnessed and are witnessing just such a reconstruction. Undoubtedly within this ferment, especially that emanating from the mass media, there are elements of fad and fashion—a thanatological "chic" as it were, having approximately the same level of import as organic gardening and home canning among the rich. And certainly one can never underestimate the capacity of American public discourse to transform "life and death matters" into passing enthusiasms. But there is, I believe, more to this activity than simply one more example of impermanent trendiness in modern life. Americans, especially affluent middle-class Americans, have been in the process of creating new or at least altered ways of thinking, believing, feeling, and acting about death and dying because they have been confronting a new "face of death." [2–3]

And if you are reading this now and thinking to yourself that these words eerily describe death and dying in your own historical moment ("fad and fashion" always gives me pause), then you begin to see why a book published in 1978 continues challenging everyone to examine how any decade's happy death movements can possibly be unique, or new, or revolutionary. Lofland wants readers to understand the history of the present, so that the next generation's death and dying activists might also comprehend the historical relationships to their own current struggle.

Relevance for Today

The Craft of Dying also productively intervenes in one of the 1970s' most unhelpful and unnecessary death and dying arguments, an argument that dogmatically persists today—i.e., that death is a taboo. If the happy death movement functioned like a true social movement, Lyn Lofland reasoned, then that movement needed an enemy, and the death taboo is the perfect foil, since everybody already "knows" that it "exists."

Lofland is neither the first author, nor will she be the last, to thoroughly challenge how and why the death taboo argument is used, abused, and greatly exaggerated. The death taboo will always be a productive fiction for various happy death movement groups committed to ideologically transforming the "face of death" in America and the West, but it is a fiction all the same. As she rightly points out in part III, the death taboo argument serves a useful function that is especially popular with death-movement intellectuals (full disclosure: I am a card-carrying member of said group). Her critique of death-movement intellectuals is reason enough to appreciate how farsighted this text remains today. Lofland's crucial intervention begins:

> It has been variously formulated, but essentially the view holds that America is a death-denying society, that death is a taboo topic, that death makes Americans uncomfortable so they run from it, that death is hidden in America because Americans deny it, and so forth. The consequences of all this denial and repression are asserted to be quite terrible: exorbitant funeral costs and barbaric funeral practices, inhumane handling of dying in hospitals, ostracism of the dying from the living, inauthentic communication with the fatally ill, an unrealistic, mechanical, non-organic view of life, and so forth. ... As many scholars have pointed out, the empirical evidence for all these assertions is something less than overwhelming (see, for example, Dumont and Foss, 1972; Donaldson, 1972). And one might consider it somewhat odd that the statement that death is a taboo topic in America should continue to be asserted in the face of nearly a decade of non-stop talking on the subject. But if one appreciates the functions these statements serve in enemy evocation, one can also appreciate that their questionable empirical basis is hardly a serious obstacle to endless repetition. The importance of the "conventional view of death"—of the conventional wisdom about death—as propounded over and over again by movement intellectuals, is not its "truth" but its utility. [71–73]

If making more people rigorously question whether or not they really need the death taboo fiction to advance their own death and dying arguments is the only thing republishing *The Craft of Dying* accomplishes, then all the waiting was worth it. Seeing the taboo argument finally debunked would also recognize Lofland's scholarly commitment to status quo challenging scholarship both then and now. That said, I have a strong hunch that in the decades to come many death-movement intellectuals and practitioners will still make the death taboo argument to advance both their careers and book sales—a point not lost on Lofland when she states that the death taboo is always about utility, not truth.

Above and beyond the book's uncanny timeliness (e.g., when reading the preface, replace all the originally listed years with the current year and note the similarities) Lofland taps into another core human experience: we *Homo sapiens* persist at dying. The fact that we all eventually die becomes that rare universal constant that allows each human the opportunity, should we take it, to experience and think about death and dying in new ways. Part II, *Individual Constructions: Styling and Controlling the Dying Role*, in particular, focuses on how the dying person becomes something different during the 1970s.

I found myself directly confronting Lofland's newly articulated experience of death and dying, as discussed in part II, when my younger sister, Julie Troyer, died from terminal brain cancer on July 29, 2018. Watching my sister die made me reflect quite heavily on *The Craft of Dying's* key assertions, and in very unexpected ways that accidentally (albeit sadly) coincided with writing this introduction. The MIT Press expressed interest in republishing *The Craft of Dying* while my sister was dying, but I started writing the introduction after she was dead—an interval of approximately one-month. My father, Ron Troyer, a long-time grief and bereavement support-group facilitator and retired American Funeral Director, best summed up my death interval experience in very Loflandian language: it is one thing to publically say, "Julie is dying," it's an entirely different experience to state, "Julie is dead." The former felt active, the latter inert.

I chose to add this section about my recent experience with death and dying, as Lofland rigorously analyzes the role of language and expressivity in encouraging people to discuss precisely these issues. For many days I wondered aloud if it was appropriate for a death studies academic, such as myself, to write a new introduction for *The Craft of Dying* that includes a discussion of such a personal experience. After staring at this book for what seemed like eons, I fully realized the genius of Lyn Lofland's irreplaceable contribution to contemporary death and dying discourse: that, no matter what any of us do; no matter our personal, professional, or familial relationship with death, everyone still dies. And that Lofland's always-new-craft-of-dying requires we living humans to critically reflect on these confrontations with mortality in our own meaningful ways, so that we might glimpse, for a moment, what living and dying can become in our technologically advanced twenty-first century. It is vitally important, I think Lofland would say, to see our personal mortal ends in the modern face of death.

What, Then, for the Future of *The Craft of Dying*?

I see no reason why this book will not remain relevant for another forty years. In surveying how *The Craft of Dying's* central arguments evolved over time, connections clearly emerge with the ACT-UP AIDS protests of the 1980s and 1990s, and the contemporary activism of today's Black Lives Matter groups. Lofland rightly predicts that death and dying social movements will persist at emerging and folding back into each other, precisely because death refuses to phenomenologically disappear. The complexity of what she wrote has never dissipated and will continue to find new audiences for many years to come. Part I, The Situation of Modern Dying: Problems and Potentials, sums up via the chapter title itself what each generation will assuredly confront.

The Craft of Dying does come with a cautionary note, however, and it is a point that bears mentioning in the conclusion to this new introduction.

Happy death movement groups (then and now) always run the risk of alienating the very people they so eagerly want to help through non-stop ultra-upbeat expressive death talking that then demands transforming and accepting death/dying/mortality at all costs. The challenge here involves individuals becoming convinced that they are doing death wrong, and in that moment of doubt, Lofland wryly suggests, a "dismal death" movement might emerge:

> If expressivity comes to be widely accepted as the only way to achieve a decent death, the emotionally reticent will find themselves under great pressure to "share." If the idea that death and dying provide new opportunities for self-improvement becomes common currency, the chronic under achiever will find himself facing one more opportunity for failure. Not "getting off" on death may become as déclassé as sexual unresponsiveness. Then perhaps, a "dismal death" movement will rise to wipe the smile from the face of death and restore the "Grim Reaper" to his historic place of honor. [86]

This book will remain relevant for all these specific cautionary reasons, and many more. I hope that in another four decades *The*

Craft of Dying is republished for that historical moment's own happy death movements; especially the ones that still evoke the death taboo enemy in order to evangelize a getting-off-on-death gospel. The irony, of course, is that Lyn Lofland showed us all how easy it is to talk about death and dying without ever transgressing any taboos, and she did this forty years ago in the book that you are about to read.

On further reflection it becomes clear that most happy death movements just can't help themselves when it comes to constantly talking about this taboo that isn't actually true. Why? It makes them feel useful. Lyn Lofland would likely say that's okay.

In the face of dying, Death doesn't really care.

Works Cited and Consulted

Donaldson, Peter J. (1972) "Denying death: a note regarding ambiguities in the current discussion." *Omega* November: 285–290.

Dumont, Richard G. and Dennis C. Foss (1972) *The American View of Death: Acceptance or Denial?* Schenkman.

United States. President's Commission for the Study of Ethical Problems in Medicine and Biomedical Behavioral Research. (1981) "Defining Death: A Report on the Medical, Legal and Ethical Issues in the Determination of Death." Government Printing Office.

United States. President's Council on Bioethics. (2009) "Controversies in the Determination of Death: A White Paper by the President's Council on Bioethics." Government Printing Office. http://bioethics.george town.edu/pcbe/reports/death/index.html.

Acknowledgments

Given the brevity of this essay, my debts are embarrassingly heavy. When I first encountered them at the University of California, San Francisco Graduate Program in Sociology in 1968, Barney Glaser and Anselm Strauss had already established themselves as pioneers in the modem *sociology* of death and dying. That I later worked in the area for several years before I consciously recognized this obvious genesis of both my interest and its particular character is testimony only to the student's typical amnesia about the influence of teachers. I am pleased publicly to acknowledge now this return of memory. Numerous persons provided invaluable assistance in the gathering of the materials that are the building blocks of this piece. I am grateful to Katherine Buckles, Ken Smith and Michael Greany for all their bibliographic work and for the patience and persistence they demonstrated; to Dorothy Place and Juanita Wood for their fine reports on various "movement" events; and to numerous students in my Sociology of Death course, to Juanita Wood and to Joan Kron for sharing with me the materials of their own research on contemporary death activities. I want also to thank six persons who generously read portions of or all the manuscript at various stages and provided useful critiques, support or

both: Sue Blanshan, Kathy Charmaz, Joan Kron, John MacDougall, Victor Marshall and Dena Robertson. Finally, I wish especially to acknowledge John Lofland for his patient prodding and
detailed editorial advice.

Grateful acknowledgment is also made for permission to
quote from the following copyrighted material:

From "When, Why, and Where People Die," by Monroe Lerner, in *The
Dying Patient*, edited by Orville G. Brim, Jr. et al., © 1970 Russell Sage
Foundation, New York.

Robert I. Levy, *Tahitians: Mind and Experience in the Society Islands*,
Chicago and London: The University of Chicago Press. © 1973 by The
University of Chicago.

Keith W. Kerr, "Death and Grief Counselling," mimeograph, 1974. Presented in part at "Alternative Death Systems in America" Conference,
University of California, Berkeley, February 21–23, 1975. Earlier version
published in *The Marriage and Family Counselors Quarterly* (Winter 1972).

Preface

The decade from mid-1960 through mid-1970 witnessed a great deal of collective bustle in the United States (and other parts of the industrial world) over death and dying. The fact that in May of 1978 *Newsweek* ran a cover story on "Living with dying" merely highlighted the enormous range of diverse activities that had absorbed the energies and attention of so many persons in the preceding years.

For example, 51% of the 133 articles indexed under "death" in the *Reader's Guide to Periodical Literature* between 1965 and mid-1975 were published in 1973 or later.

For example, in mid-1976, two "death books" (and the numbers of these published during the period were phenomenal) were included in the *New York Times Book Review* list of best-sellers: Raymond A. Moody, Jr.'s *Life After Life* and Elisabeth Kübler-Ross's *On Death and Dying,* the latter having previously achieved the status of a classic among the "thanatologically" inclined.

For example, the *New York Times* reported in 1976 that "each year since its paperback publication in 1970, *On Death and Dying* has sold a greater number of copies and has now reached a total of 1,032,000.[1]

For example, Kübler-Ross herself became something of a celebrity, her views on death reaching an audience far larger than the readers of books. *Reader's Digest* for August 1976 reprinted an interview with her condensed from two interviews, one of which originally appeared in *Family Circle* (September 1975), the other initially published in *People* (November 24, 1975).

For example, in Los Angeles, the Association for Humanistic Psychology's three-day conference on "The Art of Dying," held in November 1974, registered 450 people.

For example, in February 1975, the University of California, Berkeley offered a weekend extension course entitled "Alternative Death Systems in America." Two hundred fifty-five persons enrolled.

For example, in September 1975, *Newsweek,* reporting on the success of a new counterculture magazine called *High Times,* noted that upcoming issues were to contain fashion spreads of the Hell's Angels in T-shirts, a cover story on turquoise jewelry, an exclusive interview with the Dalai Lama, and articles on voodoo drugs, erotic art in the Vatican—and *getting high on death.*[2]

For example, a journal kept by a young Colorado woman dying of cancer became the basis for a television movie—*Sunshine*—initially shown in 1973 and later turned into a novel of the same name (Klein, 1976). Michael Roemer's film, *Dying*, was televised by PBS stations in late April of 1976. Interviews with dying persons appeared frequently in the press, as did stories with such headlines as, "Suppose you're about to die," "Some open talk about dying," "Our children facing death," "How she felt on the brink of death," "Understanding mortality: 12 experiments with dying," "Death is a personal matter," "The special needs of the dying," and "Should the dying child be told his fate?"

For example, in 1972, the Special Committee on Aging of the United States Senate—quietly and with minimal media attention—held hearings on "Death with Dignity: An Inquiry Into Related Public Issues." Since then, debates over the ethics and legal complexities of euthanasia—variously defined—moved more clearly into the arena of public discourse, crystallized and intensified, perhaps, by such long-running media events as the Karen Ann Quinlan case.

For example, in late 1974, Threshold Research Center on Death and Dying, Inc., of Los Angeles offered to the public the services of "dying companions" at the rate of $7.50 an hour, and in February, the UPI reported that Threshold's business was thriving (*The Sacramento Bee*, February 27, 1975). And in the summer of 1976 in Florida, state prison officials announced their plans for "a course and series of seminars to psychologically prepare death row inmates for the electric chair" (*The Sacramento Bee*, July 23, 1976).

In the essay that follows I want to try to make some sociological sense of some of these kinds of activities; to view a portion of these death-related doings with the "sociological eye." My focus will be on the *what* and *how* of all this collective bustle. I am concerned, that is, with such questions as: What are the important elements of the modern "face of death"? What are the important components of a modern "craft of dying"? How do the dying construct a dying role or identity for themselves? How do varying conditions intrude on the freedom of that construction? Put more generally, I will be analyzing what modern death and dying are like and how contemporary humans—individually and collectively—are dealing with them.

My focus, therefore, is not causal. That is, I shall not specifically address the question of *why* this activity emerged exactly when it did, rather than earlier or later or not at all.[3] Obviously there is implied causality in my broad linkage of the "face of death" with the "craft of dying" but this is causality at the level of sociological truism, not a detailed specification of the "conditions under which."

The materials from which this essay was constructed are diverse. Beginning in the early 1970s, I or my students attended numerous "death and dying" conferences and symposia. I have assiduously collected a considerable portion of the written material—of both a scholarly and popular character—being produced by those interested in the topic. I am a member and/or on the mailing list of many of the organizations that concern themselves with death and dying reform. And I have spoken personally to many of the individuals who express this concern. I cannot exactly claim "intimate familiarity" (J. Lofland, 1976a) with these activities. I can however, claim very close attention to them. I hope that what follows makes a contribution to that small portion of the thanatological literature that is concerned not with selling reform but with attempting to understand.

I The Situation of Modern Dying: Problems and Potentials

Like the prolonged helplessness of its young, like bisexual reproduction, the inevitable fact of death provides one of the great parameters of the human condition.[1] It can neither be "believed" nor "magicked" nor "scienced" away.[2] And while it seems possible, theoretically, for humans to act—at least for a time—as if it didn't occur, in fact, no human group of which we have any knowledge fails to take death into account. Everywhere and always humans think about it and develop beliefs regarding it and produce emotions toward it and do things relative to it. What they think, believe, feel, and do is, of course, variant. But *that* they think, believe, feel, and do is a universal. Similarly, the fact of death in human populations is a universal. But the *face of death* characteristically encountered by any given human population is variant. That is, while the "causes" and "situations" of death that can be found within any human group are likely to be diverse, each group is also likely to have a constellation or constellations of death causes and situations that are particularly characteristic for it. Does almost everyone die only when they are "old," for example, or does death come frequently to the young? Does it routinely take with it only a few members of the group on each visit or does it carry away large numbers at one time? Are the people who die spatially separated or are they often gathered together? Does death usually give notice of its coming or does it appear suddenly and unexpectedly? Is it frequently preceded by pain and physical degeneration or is high fever and unconsciousness its typical harbinger? And so on and so forth.

It seems quite probable that at least some portion of the many differences among humans in their dealing and copings with death has to do with *which* death or combinations of deaths they routinely confront. The culture and organization of death—the complex of thinkings, believings, feelings, and doings relative to it—in any given group at any given time, then, is not so much a culture and organization of universal death (although it may contain elements of such). It is, rather, a culture and organization of *characteristic* death or deaths.[3] If the latter changes, old ways of acting and feeling and thinking may seem unsatisfactory or irrelevant or inappropriate or incomplete. And while the old ways may persist despite their perceived inadequacies, it seems likely that eventually humans will construct for themselves a new, or at least altered, death culture and organization—a new "craft of dying"—better able to contain the new experience.[4]

I believe, as do other sociological observers (Charmaz, in press, for example), that in the ferment of activity relative to death and dying during the last two decades in the United States[5] we have witnessed and are witnessing just such a reconstruction. Undoubtedly within this ferment, especially that emanating from the mass media, there are elements of fad and fashion—a thanatological "chic" as it were, having approximately the same level of import as organic gardening and home canning among the rich. And certainly one can never underestimate the capacity of American public discourse to transform "life and death matters" into passing enthusiasms. But there is, I believe, more to this activity than simply one more example of impermanent trendiness in modern life. Americans, especially affluent middle-class Americans, have been in the process of creating new or at least altered ways of thinking, believing, feeling, and acting about death and dying because they have been confronting a new "face of death." I propose to explore that new face, to specify some of the problems and potentials it creates and to analyze the "constructions"—both individual and collective—it is evoking.

The Situation: The Prolongation, Bureaucratization, and Secularization of Dying

Prolongation

Humans are the sorts of creatures who know they are going to die, foreknowledge of death being one of the characteristics of the species. Whether they are unique among earth creatures in the possession of this characteristic (as is commonly assumed) or whether they share it with other living forms is neither known, nor in this instance, pertinent. It is sufficient simply to take note of humankind's notice of future death. Given such fore-knowledge, it is, as many have observed, philosophically both legitimate and accurate to say that *all* the living are "dying," and have been from the moment of birth. Despite this, human groups generally seem to distinguish rather sharply between the living and the dying. Different groups have different rules for determining who is dying, of course—different requisites for admission to the category.[6] But however various the precise rules, all human groups seem to have them. No social order appears to allow its members to enter the dying category simply "willy-nilly." In the contemporary United States, for example, it is not acceptable for a 20-year-old to claim she is dying based only on the likelihood that death will occur in 40–50 years. Nor is a soldier "dying" when he enters battle, even if the probability of his survival is very low. Nor a woman of 80 in vigorous good health, no matter her "actuarial" closeness to death. Among Americans, currently, "dying" seems, in contrast, to be a rather special category reserved for those whose bodies are said, by the appropriate experts, to be in the grips of "diseases" or conditions which, within some generally specifiable period of time, will eventuate in death.[7]

There are many aspects of "being dying" that would be fruitful to pursue but I wish to emphasize only one: duration—the length of time one can be "in" the category. Important changes in duration have occurred quite recently and a crucial new element of the dying situation in the *modern context* is the fact that "dying" is often *prolonged*. To appreciate the enormity of this change—in fact, to appreciate that a change has occurred at all—it is important to look briefly at the situation of premodern dying.[8]

Premodern Dying: The Death Encounter

Let us imagine that we wish to create a set of conditions that will ensure that the period between the onset of "dying"—between admission to the dying category—and the actual occurrence of death will, typically, be relatively brief. That is, we wish to make certain that most persons will "be dying" only a short period of time; will have, with death, a mere encounter. To maximize fully the chances of achieving this outcome our list of requisite physical and social arrangements would undoubtedly need to be extensive. But let me suggest that short of such perfection, we can *reasonably* ensure brief duration dying by combining the following six interrelated conditions:[9]

(1) a low level of medical technology;

(2) late detection of disease or fatality-producing conditions;

(3) a simple definition of death;

(4) a high incidence of mortality by acute disease;

(5) a high incidence of fatality-producing injuries;

(6) customary killing or suicide of, or fatalistic passivity toward the person, once he or she has entered the dying category.

The relationship among these conditions and between them and the duration of the dying-to-death "trajectory"[10] is neither complex nor mysterious. With a low level of medical technology (1), the capacity for effective interference with or deceleration of mortality-producing processes is minimized and the likelihood that such processes will be "detected" close to the death end of the trajectory (2) is maximized, thus ensuring, by definition, that the "dying" will not "be dying" very long. A low level of medical technology (1) also necessitates that the "signs of death" taken to be definitive be relatively gross and thus detectable by the unaided senses or by the senses aided only by primitive instruments. Such a simple definition of death (3) in turn facilitates brief-duration dying because it admits persons to the "dead end" of the trajectory so easily. So too, if a goodly proportion of the population dies by means of diseases or injuries that themselves bring on death rapidly (4) and (5), especially under conditions of feeble ameliorative capacities (1), "being dying" for that proportion must necessarily be attenuated. And if admission to the dying category itself engenders action or inaction that hastens or at least fails to hinder death (6), then the time spent "in the category" will likely be short. Taken together, then, in simultaneous operation, these six conditions cannot guarantee that *every* human being will make a rapid exit. But they can ensure that the *typical* dying scenario will not be a long one.

The above is only a logical model, of course, but available evidence suggests that until very recently these conditions were, in fact, present (to a greater or lesser degree) in all human societies. And some are still present in a few. Let us take, as a not unrepresentative example of dying in the premodern world, a description of the course of that disease known as the "plague" that so ravished, among other periods and locales, fourteenth-century Europe.

> The plague did not attack all people in the same way. Some retired at night, apparently well, and were found dead next morning; some fell into a deep sleep from which they could not be roused; some were struck suddenly and died within a few hours; others, wild with fever, could not sleep and were consumed with a deadly thirst. It was not uncommon for persons who felt no pain to see the tokens [dark spots which appeared on the breast or back] and then be dead in a few hours. Dr. Hodges ... says that men who were engaged in conversation with their friends have been known to fall suddenly into a profound and often deadly sleep. Dr. Guthrie, who was in Moscow during one visit of the plague, saw men fall as if shot ... some of these however, would recover. Dr. Alexander Russell ... confirms these reports and Antes ... has known men to drop dead without the least warning sign.
>
> It must not be inferred that the majority died suddenly, i.e., without warning; those who began with nose-bleeding or blood-spitting might live a day, but not longer. If they were attacked in some other way they might live till the third day, the day on which most deaths occurred; one who lived beyond the third day was likely to die the fifth if he died at all ... [Gowen, 1907: 6]

Acute diseases, if they kill, do so with relative speed. The plague is such a disease. Note that Gowen makes no mention here of attempted intervention. The portrait he paints is one of passivity and helplessness in the face of an unknown and overwhelming force. This is not a distortion of omission. One author estimates that the bubonic plague was probably fatal to 90% or more of these infected (Nohl, 1961, quoted in Kastenbaum and Aisenberg, 1972: 196). And what Kastenbaum and Aisenberg note about medieval Europe's capacities to cope with the disease is equally valid for other places, other populations, other times. "The medieval death system was unable to offer an effective technological defense. Most medical and quasi-medical procedures were completely useless; the necessary sanitation methods were not comprehended" (Kastenbaum and Aisenberg, 1972: 197). Note also in the Gowan portrait how frequent and apparently unsurprising is late "detection" of the disease. Note in sum how some of the varying conditions for short-duration dying express themselves in the real world.

Certainly the plague—bubonic or otherwise—was not the major source of death in the premodern world, although one might have difficulty exaggerating its importance. During its fourteenth-century visitation to Europe it is estimated to have killed some 25 million persons, one-fourth to one-third of the continent's population (Goldscheider, 1976: 170). But that particular infestation was simply one of multitudes. In the single year of 1625, for example, of the 54,265 burials in the City of London, 35,417 died of plague (Wrigley, 1969: 114; see also McNeill, 1976). As Gowan notes, "From the time of the first recorded pestilence down to the present there have been comparatively few periods of any considerable length when pestilences or other epidemics have not prevailed in some part of the world. One of the most persistent of these is the disease now known as the Oriental or bubonic plague" (1907: 1). While the plague may not have been a major *source* of death in the premodern world, as a *form* of death—involving communicability and acute illness—it was apparently relatively typical. Historical cause-of-death statistics are not readily available, of course, but the experience of the so-called developing countries is thought to duplicate to some degree the historical situation, and in this experience, "communicable," "infectious," "acute" diseases predominate.[11] [condition (4)]

> Hillery et al. (1968), comparing recent mortality data from forty-one countries, have shown that the communicable diseases ("infectious diseases" in their terminology) as causes of death decline significantly as a proportion of all deaths in each country as these countries move "up" in the demographic transition, that is, as their birth and death rates decline, and as they concomitantly become at least presumably more "advanced" technologically and socially. Thus, in the "transition" countries (low death rates but high birth rates), communicable diseases account for about one-third of all deaths on the average, while in the demographically "mature" countries (both death rates and birth rates low), the comparable proportion is about one in twelve of all deaths. This finding is generally in conformity with past experience in this country [the United States] and elsewhere ... [Lerner, 1970: 15][12]

Infectious, acute diseases were an important source of death in the premodern world; so too must fatality-producing injuries have been. The evidence here is even less extensive and direct than for acute diseases but it is, I think, persuasive. Lerner, for example, reports that judging from the many skulls found with marks of blows, violence was probably the usual cause of death during prehistory (1970: 7). And from what we know of wars, natural calamities, feuds, riots, rough sport, executions, construction techniques, the prevalence of fire, contact with animals, and travel capacities and dangers throughout history[13] we can quite legitimately deduce that for large numbers of our ancestors, dying as well as living was mean, brutish, and *short*. [condition (5)]

It is important to emphasize once again that these important causes of death are operating under conditions of a low level of medical technology. Goldscheider speaks of preindustrial mortality as "uncontrolled directly" (1976: 166–167), meaning that the fluctuating mortality patterns prior to the eighteenth century were not being created, except indirectly and unwittingly, by human hands. Mortality was the consequence, of course, of "general social, economic, political and cultural conditions" and these were themselves human productions. And certainly deaths that resulted from intentional actions were controlled deaths. But in general, men and women were not consciously or intentionally altering or shaping their mortality experience: they had neither the knowledge nor the technology to do so. [condition (1)]

Critics of modern death orientations frequently evoke an idealized past in which death is said to have been "accepted."[14] Given human impotence relative to its control, one could as well speak of "fatalism" and "passivity." Among some human groups, if a member were dying, death was deliberately induced. Simmons reports, for example that

> among the Samoans the aged were buried alive at their own request. It was even considered a disgrace to the family of an aged chief if he were not so honored. "When an old man felt sick and infirm and thought he was dying, he deliberately told his children and friends to get all ready and bury him. They yielded to his wishes, dug a round deep pit, wound a number of fine mats. around his body, and

lowered down the poor old man into his grave in a sitting posture. ... His grave was filled up, and his dying groans drowned amid the weeping and wailing of the living."...

It was a tradition among the Yakut that in ancient times, if a person became extremely decrepit, or if anyone became ill beyond hope of recovery, he generally begged his beloved children or relatives to bury him. Then the neighbors were called together, the best and fattest cattle were slaughtered, and a three-day feast was celebrated. ... At the conclusion of the ceremonies the relatives chosen by him led him into the wood and suddenly thrust him into a hole previously prepared. [Simmons, 1945: 236–237]

Killing of or suicide by the dying, especially the aged dying, while not rare practices, have probably not been common among human groups. But neglect or abandonment or simple watchful comforting of the dying have been (Simmons, 1945). [condition (6)] The Tahitian scene witnessed by Robert Levy may be archetypical of the premodern dying situation.

I had been in Piri about two weeks when, one evening, Teri'i Tui Vahine said that Távana Vahine was very ill. I went down to Távana's house at the seaward end of the village to see what was happening. Távana Vahine was lying on a mattress on the floor of a large shed. ... It was crowded with twelve adults and sixteen children and young adolescents. The adults were Távana Vahine's sisters and brothers, her and Távana's grown children and some of these people's spouses. The children were her grandchildren.

When I approached the house there was loud, animated talking, joking and laughter coming from it. It resembled a festive family party, and little notice was apparently being taken of Távana Vahine, lying off in one corner. Her "favorite" daughter, Hama Vahine, sat next to her at the head of the mat, preparing compresses of cloth soaked in cold water, which she applied to her mother's head.

Távana Vahine was fully alert and aware. I went over to talk to her, and she took my hand and held onto it, looking very frightened and anxious for help. She had been having severe chest pains for several months, and had had several fainting spells during the day. Now she had pain in her chest and abdomen and pain in her left arm. Her lips were blue and her legs were swollen. She was obviously gravely ill.

During the next two or three hours the adults continued their joking conversation. ... The youngest children were asleep, but the elder children made a ring of quiet spectators, watching the conversation and the dying woman. ... As the evening went on, the elder people continued their talking with Távana actively participating and seldom glancing over at his wife.

Távana Vahine was clearly in great distress but showed it only in her clenched hands and in her frightened but whispered and controlled remarks to Hama Vahine, describing where she felt pain and where Hama Vahine should apply the cold compresses. From time to time one of Távana Vahine's other daughters, and at one time one of her brothers, went over to her and knelt by the mattress to massage her legs. As they did this, they participated in the general conversation, restraining most of their interaction with Távana Vahine to the mechanical act of massage. Távana Vahine did not moan, cry out, or complain. She was dying in a restrained, low-key, matter-of-fact way. ... There was only one time that the adults seemed to react directly to Távana Vahine's situation. She suddenly vomited, and the men sitting around the table and the women at the sides became quiet. They looked down at the floor or off into space, avoiding looking at one another. After a few minutes when Távana Vahine became quiet again, they continued their conversation.

Late at night, I went back to Teri'i Tui's to get some sleep. When I awoke, Teri'i Tui Vahine told me that Távana Vahine had died. [Levy, 1973: 291–293]

What little evidence there is,[15] suggests that like Távana Vahine, most humans admitted to the dying category throughout human history and prehistory have probably been "sick unto death." The absence of medical gadgetry, the absence of a well-developed complex medical establishment, the absence of theories of living and dying that would promote attempts at "early diagnosis," the absence of bureaucratic control of large populations, all contributed to the likelihood that diseases or potentially fatal conditions would be "identified" rather late in the dying-to-death trajectory, and this would be even more true of those who died from what are now conceived as chronic or degenerative diseases than of those who died from the more typical maladies. [condition (2)] Thus, whether a person was "dying" or not was, in the premodern world, probably minimally problematic.

Less so, however, the question of whether or not a person was dead. While the exact criteria for determining death's presence varied across time and space, until very recent times those criteria have been relatively simple and straightforward, necessarily apparent without the aid of complex instrumentation: the cessation of heart beat, for example, or of breathing, the appearance of rigor mortis, pallor, relaxation of the sphincter, and so forth (Mant, 1976: 224). [condition (3)] The actual extent to which such a simple definition of death foreshortened the dying-to-death trajectory is unknown. It seems clear, however, that the fear or suspicion that it might has bedeviled humans in many times and places. Premature burial or entombment is the stuff of widespread myth and legend and tale. Mant reports that, historically, in Europe, "the morbid fear of premature burial prompted some persons to order in their wills that before burial death must be proved surgically by incision or by the application of boiling liquids or a red hot iron to the skin. Some even demanded that they be decapitated before burial" (1976: 225). And Hendin notes, many of the works of the medicolegalists in the 1800s that listed the signs of death and warned of the potentials for error

> were prompted by the fear, common in those days, of premature burial or autopsy and cases of suspended animation. Several ingenious

gentlemen invented "indicators" to help determine whether a person had indeed been buried alive. The devices were often complicated gadgets to be placed in the grave. They would raise a flag or sound a warning in case the casket's occupant stirred. It was the macabre fear of being buried alive, as well as a fear of cruelty in burying others alive, that to a large extent prompted men to seek more information concerning the determination of death.

In 1890, the Prix Dusgate, a prize of twenty-five hundred francs, was awarded to Dr. Maze who, in his belief that putrefaction was the only sure sign of death, advocated that cemeteries provide mortuaries where the bodies of deceased could lie until putrefaction began, thus eliminating all possibilities of mistaken burial. [Hendin, 1973: 22–23]

I have been arguing here that until quite recently the conditions that produce brief-duration dying have been empirically present throughout most of the world and that as a consequence, for large numbers of humans, dying has characteristically involved only a short span of time. Between admission to the category dying and extinction, most of our ancestors, I would suggest, confronted only minutes or hours or days. And even when their dying took longer, the high incidence of acute disease would have rendered many of them delirious or unconscious during much of the course of the last illness, such that their participation in "being dying" would necessarily have been forestalled. Certainly, as numerous scholars have noted, in the premodern world, death was generally a much greater experiential constant than it is today (for example, Blauner, 1966; Goldscheider, 1971, 1976; Kastenbaum and Aisenberg, 1972). Throughout his or her life span, the average individual confronted a continuous procession of *others' deaths*. Nonetheless, and rather oddly, the confrontation with his or her *own death* was likely to be a mere encounter.

Modern Dying: The Death Affair

If the dying situation of the premodern human can be likened to an encounter, the dying situation for more and more modern humans is best viewed as a full-blown affair.[16] To understand why this should be the case, let us consider six conditions—parallel to those we considered above—that might facilitate the prolongation of dying:

(1) a high level of medical technology;

(2) early detection of disease or fatality-producing conditions;

(3) a complex definition of death;

(4) a high incidence of mortality by chronic or degenerative disease;

(5) a low incidence of fatality-producing injuries;

(6) customary curative and activist orientation toward the dying with a high value placed on the prolongation of life.

Again, the interrelationships are straightforward. With a high level of medical technology (1), the capacity for effective interference with or deceleration of mortality-producing processes is maximized, as is the likelihood that such processes will be detected far from the death end of the trajectory (2), thus ensuring, by definition, that the dying will be dying for some period. A high level of medical technology (1) also makes it possible for the signs of death taken to be definitive to be relatively complex and subtle since they can depend on extremely sensitive instrumentation. A complex definition of death (3) in turn facilitates prolonged dying because it admits persons to the dead end of the trajectory so selectively. So too, if a goodly proportion of the population dies primarily by means of diseases that themselves bring on death slowly (4) and (5)—especially under conditions of strong ameliorative capacities (1)—"being dying" for that proportion will necessarily be prolonged. And if admission to the dying category itself engenders highly valued actions that postpone death (6), then the time spent in the category will likely be increased. Taken together, then, in simultaneous operation, these six conditions cannot guarantee that *every* human being will make a prolonged exit. But they can ensure that the *typical* dying scenario will not be brief.

In fact, in the real modern world, not all of these conditions are present or present in sufficient strength to ensure absolutely that prolonged dying will be the experience of the majority. But *enough* of the conditions are present in sufficient strength for the words of an anonymous American published in the *Atlantic Monthly* in the late 1950s to stand for the experience of a large proportion of Americans in the late 1970s.

> There is a new way of dying today. It is the slow passage via modern medicine. If you are very ill, modern medicine can save you. If you are going to die, it can prevent you from so doing for a very long time. ... Enter the sickroom and sit with your beloved and endure the long watch while this incredible battle between spirit and medicine takes place. It may continue for weeks, sometimes for months. But the victim is going to die. It is just a question of time. Every new formula, all the latest wonder drugs, the tricks and artificial wizardry, are now prescribed and brought to bear. [Anonymous, 1957]

Something of this modern experience is reflected also in the dying of the husbands whose widows Lopata has studied, as reported in Tables I.1 and I.2. More than half of these husbands were ill from three months to over a year before their deaths (Table I.1). And, not surprisingly and characteristically, more than 60% succumbed to either heart disease or cancer (Table I.2).

Not the plague, not "intermittent fevers," not diptheria or smallpox[17] or typhoid or influenza dominate the modern

Table I.1
Length of Time Husband Did Not Work Full-time Because of Last Illness

Length of Time	Percent
None to 8 weeks	47.4
3 mos. to 1 year or more	52.6
N = 19 2	

Table I.2
Cause of Husband's Death

	Percent	
Accident	3.4	
Heart disease	47.1	} 64.3
Cancer	17.2	
Stroke	6.2	
Diabetes	2.1	
Combined	2.7	
Other	17.5	
N = 291		

Source: Condensed from Helen Znaniecki Lopata, *Widowhood in an American City* (1973: 310).

death experience. For contemporary humans, death frequently approaches not with the youthful step of acute illness but with the shuffle of chronic or degenerative disease. [condition (4)] Shibles notes that "from 1900 to 1956 in the United States, death from pneumonia and other infectious diseases, which caused death mainly before age 35, fell but deaths from cardiovascular-renal disease and cancer rose" (1974: 508). And Lerner points up the fact that one of the most significant changes in the mortality experience of this country since 1900 has been the decline in the major communicable diseases as leading causes of death and the consequent increase in *relative importance* of the so-called chronic degenerative diseases, that is diseases occurring mainly later in life and generally thought to be associated in some way with the aging process. [1970: 12–13]

These generalizations are graphically presented in Table I.3.[18]

A high incidence of death from chronic and degenerative diseases does not, of course, guarantee prolonged dying. Diseases of the heart remain the primary cause of death in the United States, and these often kill suddenly and without warning. In fact, Lerner believes that the short time interval between onset of the condition and death is one of the reasons why a relatively small proportion of heart-disease-related deaths occur in hospitals (1970: 26). But heart diseases can be, in themselves, slow killers—and cancer certainly is. And to the degree that the slow killers are an important element in the death profile of a people, so much more will prolonged dying be facilitated. At the moment both heart disease and accidents [condition (5)] remain too high in the lexicon of death causes in the United States for the maximally facilitating strengths of the death-cause conditions to obtain (although recent evidence suggests that death rates from heart diseases and accidents are dropping while the rate for cancer is climbing[19]). Additionally, acute diseases remain of some importance as causes of death among lower class groups, further diluting the strength of the conditions' presence (Anonymous, 1968). Nonetheless, the great drift is clearly in the direction of more and more deaths being caused by processes that themselves play out slowly.

These chronic or degenerative diseases—both those that are inherently rapid and those that are inherently slow in their

Table I.3

The Ten Leading Causes of Death, by Rank, United States, 1900 and 1966

1900

Rank	Cause of Death	Deaths Per 100,000 Population	Percent of all Deaths
	All causes	1,719.1	100.0
1	Influenza and pneumonia	202.2	11.8
2	Tuberculosis (all forms)	194.4	11.3
3	Gastritis, duodenitis, enteritis, etc.	142.7	8.3
4	Diseases of the heart	137.4	8.0
5	Vascular lesions affecting the central nervous system	106.9	6.2
6	Chronis nephritis	81.0	4.7
7	All accidents	72.3	4.2
8	Malignant neoplasms (cancer)	64.0	3.7
9	Certain diseases of early infancy	62.6	3.6
10	Diphtheria	40.3	2.3

1966

Rank	Cause of Death	Deaths Per 100,000 Population	Percent of all Deaths
	All causes	954.2	100.0
1	Diseases of the heart	375.1	39.3
2	Malignant neoplasms (cancer)	154.8	16.2
3	Vascular lesions affecting the central nervous system	104.6	11.0
4	All accidents	57.3	6.0
5	Influenza and pneumonia	32.8	3.4
6	Certain diseases of early infancy	26.1	2.7
7	General arteriosclerosis	19.5	2.0
8	Diabetes mellitus	18.1	1.9
9	Cirrhosis of the liver	13.5	1.4
10	Suicide	10.3	1.1

Source: From Monroe Lerner, "When, Why, and Where People Die" (1970: 14).

march toward death—reach prominence in the mortality experience of the modern world enveloped, penetrated, poked, and produced by a medical technology almost unbelievable in its extent. The United States, as an advanced industrialized nation is, of course, technologically enormously sophisticated and, unsurprisingly, its medical sector participates in that sophistication.[20] [condition (1)] The panoply of "wonder drugs, tricks and artificial wizardry" available to medicine is too well known to require elucidation here.[21] Suffice to say that the technology's capacities for interference with and deceleration of mortality-producing processes have attained such heights that questions are now being raised about whether all that prolongation and deceleration is truly desirable.[22]

Conversely, the technology's successes with early detection of diseases or fatality-producing conditions [condition (2)] have generated complaints that not enough is being done in this direction or that not enough people utilize the detection devices available[23] or that even more extensive control of the citizenry by the medical bureaucracy is required. The technology's successes have also massively complicated the formerly relatively straightforward (as we have seen, *too* straight-forward for some) matter of when death occurs. New devices (heart-lung machines, for example) and sensitive instrumentation have shifted attention away from such fairly simple issues of whether a body is breathing or a heart beating, to the complex issue of whether a brain is still functioning. There is simply no question but that, given increasing utilization of modern definitions of death, many humans are currently dying who fifty years ago would already be dead.[24] [condition (3)] The impact of technological wonders is not, of course, self-created. Technology intersects with ongoing social arrangements only if it is used. In this instance, the same values and practices that created medical wizardry in the first place ensure its utilization. The American medical establishment as well as important segments of the nation state's general population unquestionably take a strongly curative and activist orientation toward the dying because they place a very high value on the prolongation of life.[25] [condition (6)]

I am arguing that in the last several hundred years, more importantly in the last fifty years, and even more importantly in the last twenty years, conditions have emerged with sufficient strength to produce in the modern world a new kind of dying—prolonged dying—which relatively large numbers of persons have confronted, are now confronting, or will confront. Between admission to the category dying and extinction, more and more persons are confronting—and doing so consciously—not minutes or hours or days but weeks or months or even years. As we shall see, this prolongation of the dying-to-death trajectory is a source of problems. It is also a source of potentials.

Bureaucratization and Secularization

Two further characteristics of the contemporary dying situation are important to note. Modern dying is not only, frequently, prolonged; that prolongation is occurring, importantly, within a context that is both bureaucratized and secularized. For significant numbers of modern humans, the "death affair" is—at least intermittently—being played out within an institutional environment—primarily the hospital. And it is being played out within a milieu of beliefs and understandings and knowings that offer little if any clues to its teleological meaning.

As Blauner has insightfully pointed out, there is nothing at all peculiar about the fact that modern societies should handle death and dying bureaucratically[26] since

> bureaucratization [is] our characteristic form of social structure. Max
> Weber has described how bureaucratization in the West proceeded
> by removing social functions from the family and the household and
> implanting them in specialized institutions autonomous of kinship
> considerations. Early manufacturing and entrepreneurship took place
> in or close to the home; modern industry and corporate bureaucracies
> are based on the separation of the workplace from the household.
> [Blauner, 1966: 384]

Evidence that would provide a detailed portrait of the intersec-
tion of "being dying" and the institutional setting—that would
inform us of the frequency and duration of the medical bureaucracy experiences of those defined as dying—is neither easily nor
readily available. But we can get some sense of the broad outlines
by looking at where "death" occurs. Morrison (1973) argues that,
in New York City, in the relatively brief period between 1955 and
1967 there was a discernible increase in deaths in institutions,
and that even in 1955, deaths in institutions accounted for over
60% of the total. Lerner reports on the situation nationally.

> From national data ... it seems clear that the proportion of all deaths
> in this country occurring in institutions has been rising steadily, at
> least for the last two decades and probably for much longer than that.
> It may now be as high as, or higher than, two-thirds of all deaths. ...
> In 1958, according to the most recent *national* data available, 60.9
> percent of all deaths in this country occurred in institutions, that
> is, in hospitals, convalescent and nursing homes, and in hospital
> departments of institutions or in other domiciliary institutions. This
> figure represented a considerable rise over the comparable 49.5 per-
> cent recorded in 1949, the most recent preceding year for which a
> national tabulation was made. On the basis of these data it appeared
> that the proportion was rising by an average of better than 1 percent
> annually.
>
> National data to test whether the trend continued beyond that
> year are unavailable, but state and local data appear to indicate that
> this, in fact, may have been the case. In New York City, for example,

the proportion of deaths occurring in institutions rose steadily, with only one very slight fluctuation, from 65.9 percent in 1955 to 73.1 percent in 1967. ... Data from the Maryland State Department of Health also indicate a substantial upward progression in the proportion of all deaths occurring in institutions, from 64.4 percent in 1957 to 71.8 percent in 1966.

Most of the deaths occurring in "institutions" ... occurred in hospitals, the vast majority of which were general hospitals. [Lerner, 1970: 7, 21–22]

Finally, modern dying, like modern living, takes place within a profoundly secular context—upsurges in the popularity of sacred fads notwithstanding. There exists currently no widely accepted, fully articulated, well-integrated dogma that gives "being dying" its meaning or its place in the larger scheme of things.[27] As such, the secularization of dying, like its prolongation and bureaucratization, creates both problems and potentials for those affected. It is to a consideration of such problems and potentials that we now turn.

Problems and Potentials

The situation of modern dying creates three clusters of problems and potentials. It creates a cluster relative to the dying role in raising the question "how shall I act?" It creates a second cluster relative to organizational arrangements for coping with dying in raising the question "what shall we do?" And it creates a third cluster relative to beliefs about death and dying in raising the question "what does it mean?"

Role Problems and Potentials: "How Shall I Act?"

As we have seen, for large numbers of humans in the premodern world, the question of what to do when facing personal death—how to act—was not a question that required a very involved or complex answer. The period of time available for *doing anything* was simply too short.[28] That is, one can speak of the "dying role" in the premodern world only in a very tangential or marginal sense—only in the sense that, for example, one might speak of an airplane passenger "role" in a social order in which no one flew more than once and all trips were of short duration. It is only very recently that any significant portion of human beings find themselves "dying" for a long enough period of time for the issue of how best to go about it meaningfully to be raised. That a new role possibility—that a new "core category" (J. Lofland, 1969) around which identity may be formed—has emerged and that this new role possibility is unencumbered by much historic structuring, engenders action problems for those who take it on. It also engenders potentials for the creative combining of identity construction materials. We shall explore in part II, some of the ways individual modern actors have chosen to meet these challenges.

Organizational Problems and Potentials: "What Shall We Do?"

The fact that dying is, in the modern world, handled "characteristically," that is, with a bureaucratic form of social organization,[29] does not guarantee that either the bureaucratic handling generally or specific bureaucratic arrangements will be perceived as satisfactory. As we have seen, the prolonged dying constitute a growing but relatively new group of hospital clientele. Most hospitals were designed not for them but for those defined as "recoverable." Thus the presence in these settings of a group for whom the settings were not designed generates both problems (for example, staff frustration or client dissatisfaction) and potentials (for example, new organizational forms). In part

III we shall explore examples of collective responses to these challenges.

Belief Problems and Potentials: "What Does It Mean?"

Contributors to the "death literature" are fond of repeating de la Rochefoucauld's epigram: "One cannot look directly at either the sun or death." Yet, in fact, prolonged dying, handled bureaucratically, often necessitates that three groups of persons—the dying, their intimates, and relevant bureaucratic personnel (for example, nurses, aides, attendants, social workers, chaplains, physicians)—look fairly directly at death for fairly long periods of time. In the main, they have been doing so unarmed with any traditional certainties about deities, afterlives, or universal schemes. In a secular age, the population that is most likely to confront prolonged dying either occupationally or personally is also—ironically enough—as relatively affluent, educated moderns, most likely to have discarded the beliefs that might have imbued that confrontation with meaning.[30] Yet if we know anything about humans, we know that they do not confront meaningless situations for very long. In the face of meaninglessness, they construct for themselves new sets of beliefs, new orientations, new ways of looking or feeling that fill the void. Also in part III we shall be inspecting one such collective effort at meaning construction.

Before turning to an analysis of dying identity construction activities, however, a final observation is in order. If there has, in fact, been a period in American history in which, as many commentators insist, death and dying seemed to be ignored in public discourse, the explanation for such a hiatus does not have to rest on evocations of taboos, death fears, avoidance reactions, and so forth.[31] Such a hiatus might be accounted for as follows.

From the nineteenth century on, but increasingly and more rapidly into the twentieth, the demographics of death undergo important changes. Gradually, the phenomenon of prolonged dying emerges. Characteristically, it is dealt with bureaucratically. Increasingly, more and more of the dying are dying in hospitals rather than at home. But there is a time lag before the number of persons who are confronting death (the occupational group, the prolonged dying, and their intimates) can reach critical mass and allow those involved to recognize and articulate their situation and/or felt dissatisfactions. That is, for a period, death and dying *do* disappear from public discourse because for large numbers of persons for most of their lives, death is not *salient* (since they will mostly die when they are older and those who are dying are organizationally segregated) and the group for whom it is very salient is neither large enough nor aware enough to articulate its concerns.

Once that group reaches sufficient size, however, it becomes aware of itself as a group and can begin publicly to articulate those concerns that its individual members had kept private. The hiatus on death and dying as public discourse ends. The emergence of death and dying as fad, fashion, and social movement begins.[32]

II Individual Constructions: Styling and Controlling the Dying Role

How to "be dying," how to act en route to the grave, is an issue with that more and more modern humans are confronted. There is little traditional wisdom to guide them, few maps to show the way. In the main, unless they choose to avoid the entire issue by "passing" (see below), they must engage in a kind of "role enterprise,"[1] constructing for themselves the particular combination of components that will make up their identities as dying persons.[2] Before proceeding to an analysis of the more activist matters of shaping (or styling) and managing (or controlling) the dying role or identity, however, we need to consider three matters of a more structural or "given" character: the aspects of *singularity*, *entry*, and *phases*.

All roles or identities can be viewed as both similar to and different from all other roles or identities, the exact nature of the similarities and differences depending on which categories the analyst considers relevant. Leaving aside questions of exhaustive topographic mapping, let me point up three ways in which "dying" is *singular*. As a way of "being" in the modern world, dying is (1) transitional, (2) irreversible, and (3) characterized by an absence of "graduates." It is (1) transitional in the dictionary sense of "being in the act or state of passing from one place, condition or action to another." As we saw in part I, contemporary usage of the category "dying" precludes one being in that category indefinitely. Only those born dying can spend their brief lifetimes in role. For most of us, it is merely a status passage.[3]

(2) Many transitional roles, especially in modern societies, contain large elements of voluntarism relative to passage completion. One may or may not finish high school, for example, one may or may not bring a pregnancy to full term, one may or may not finish a transsexual transformation by accepting surgery, and so forth. Dying, however, like aging is irreversible and coercive (Glaser and Strauss, 1971: 14–17; Marshall, 1975c). Completing the trajectory, finishing up dead, is the inevitable consequence of having "truly" entered the role in the first place, regardless of what one might prefer. Persons do, of course, appear to enter the role and then leave it, as when someone who has been defined as dying recovers. Under such circumstances, however, the initial definition is simply seen as having been erroneous. One may have been near death but one was not truly dying. To be truly dying, one must, within a reasonable period of time, have the good taste actually to die. (3) Many transitional roles or identities, whether characterized by voluntary or coercive passage, also have graduates—persons who have gone the whole route and can provide counsel, cautionary tales, instructions, and so forth to others who are still "in transit." Dying, however, like old age, lacks an alumni group; it is characterized, rather, by an absence of such graduates.[4] Persons in transit can get advice from those further on down the trajectory, but the real veterans are simply not available. As a nursing home resident notes: "Well, I don't see no future ... just death. That's all. Well, I don't

know about death. It's a puzzle. Nobody's ever come back to tell us ..." (Gubrium, 1975: 200).[5]

Entry is a second aspect of the dying role that requires discussion. In the modern world, dying shares with such dissimilar identities as university student and automobile driver the fact that entry is guarded by gate-keepers[6] who monitor prospective entrants and make decisions about whether or not they qualify for admission. From what scanty evidence is available (for example, Simmons, 1945), there is some reason to believe that in the past and perhaps in some groups still today, if certain other conditions obtain—certain omens, for example, or biological signs—one could become "dying" in the same manner one becomes a stamp collector—simply by announcing that one had done so. This is not to say that admission was unregulated. It is simply to note that actors in such groups presumably were thought to be in the position adequately to make their own judgments about their eligibility. The anthropological literature on Samoa, as an example, contains a description of a man who believed he had been told by a spirit that his death was close at hand. Although he had been in good health that morning, he left his work, returned home, and lay down on a mat in preparation for death. His family and neighbors gathered around him while he gave his final instructions and then gave himself up to death (Stair, 1897). In the contemporary United States, however, only the expert gate-keeper—primarily M.D.s, especially those who are specialists in whatever disease or condition is thought to be the killer—may pronounce that dying has begun, an arrangement that allows for the very strange situation of actors being "admitted" to the category, of their kin being so informed, but of notice of this identity change being withheld from the new entrants. It is this situation, of course, that Glaser and Strauss (1965b) have analyzed as a "closed awareness context"; a situation that creates a Kafkaesque world for its central actor and that generally breaks down after a time into suspicion or mutual pretense.[7] Another possibility exists: the actor is admitted to the role, is told of that admission, but refuses either to "hear" or believe; that is, he or she simply denies that the new category is at all applicable.[8] Both of these situations are interesting in their own right as analytic foci. But they shall not be of concern in what follows. In looking at the styling and controlling of dying roles, we shall be doing so only under the conditions that (1) actors have been fully informed of admission by gate-keepers defined as legitimate, and (2) actors accept the admission as accurate: they now consider themselves to be, in fact, dying persons. Even within these restrictive conditions, however, as we shall see, a good deal of leeway remains for playing out the dying role.

Finally, a word about dying *phases* or stages. As analysts have come to appreciate the relatively prolonged period in which modem persons can "be dying," they have begun to attempt to conceive that experience in terms of phases or stages. Kübler-Ross's (1969) "denial, anger, bargaining, depression, and acceptance" is undoubtedly the most famous formulation, but there have been many others, as well as criticisms and reformulations of the Kübler-Ross proposal.[9] Many of these attempts have been the work of psychologists or psychiatrists and as Charmaz (1976a) has noted, these have been shaped by the "unfolding" or "developmental model" predilections of their creators. In the main also, the formulations have emerged out of predominantly ameliorative concerns. That is, one articulates a set of stages—usually ending with a "good one"—so as to help the dying "get through" them. I do not want to underestimate the value of a temporal perspective in thinking about and analyzing the activities of actors who are in the dying role. It seems very likely that the shapings and managings that emerge at one point in the trajectory will often be altered—sometimes deliberately, sometimes by changing circumstances—at later points. In the current analysis, however, temporality may safely be ignored, the distortion thereby induced being minimal.

With these structural parameters in mind, let us turn to an examination of the individual fashionings by dying persons of their own dying craft.

Shaping the Role: The Problem of Style

Once they have generated a category of kind of person or being in the world, social groups tend also to generate accompanying conceptions or "cultural scripts" that provide some specification for how one is to act when one is "in" the category.[10] Speaking ideal-typically, among traditional groups, such scripts tended to be singular and specific. For many, in fact, what to do when dying seems to have been quite thoroughly scripted. Of course, since dying, as we have seen, was usually a short-term way of being, it is understandable that what one was supposed to "do" while in the category were not things anyone could do for any prolonged period of time. Consider, for example, the legendary description of a "proper" dying for a Knight of the Round Table who has the misfortune not to be able to do it in bed:

> When Launcelot, wounded and dazed in a deserted forest, realized that he had "lost even the strength of his body," he believed he was about to die. So what did he do? His gestures were fixed by old customs, ritual gestures which must be carried out *when one* is *dying.* He removed his weapons and lay down quietly upon the ground. ... He spread his arms out, his body forming a cross. ... But he remembered

to lie in such a way that his head faced east, toward Jerusalem. [Ariès, 1974b: 7–8, emphasis added][11]

In contrast, in modern social orders, dying scripts—if they can be said to exist at all—tend to be individualistic, varied, emergent and uncodified. If, therefore "being dying" is relatively problematic to those who take it on, it is not so only because as a kind of prolonged being it is of recent origin. Being dying is relatively problematic also because it is a role in the modern world, and such roles are frequently more akin to improvisational theater than to traditional drama. Parameters of some sort may be "given" (for example, the parameters of entry certification and of the necessity actually to die mentioned above), but within those, the actor has considerable freedom to shape the role's detailed stylistic enactment as he or she sees fit.[12] Therein lies some of the problem; therein lies some of the potential.

In attempting to understand some of the decisions real people in the real world have been making relative to these problems and potentials, I have found it useful to view these decisions as involving four dimensions of choice. I should like to suggest that in shaping their dyings, in developing their styles of "passing on," men and women work with, among other possible *construction materials,* the dimensions of *space, population, knowledge,* and *stance.*[13]

Space
By space, I refer to the amount of "area" within what we might conceive as the individual's total "life space" he or she chooses to devote to the dying role. What part of the pie, as it were, is to be labeled "dying"; what proportion of the self is this identity to encompass. Logically, one can imagine gradations all the

way from 100% to 0%; empirically, it seems meaningful to speak only of centrality or marginality.

The journalist, Stewart Alsop appears to have chosen the centrality option. Almost from the moment he first entered a hospital with mysterious symptoms, he began entering his experiences and feelings and, eventually, technical descriptions of his "enemy" and its progress in a journal. Two years later and a short time before his death, extracts from that journal combined with other materials were published as a book, *Stay of Execution: A Sort of Memoir*. In between, Alsop had returned intermittently to his work as a political writer. But it was the process of his dying and his *persona* as a dying person and the others who surrounded him as a dying person that filled his life space. In the book's preface, he gives some hint as to why this should have been so.

> This is, in short, a mixed-up sort of book. But I have led a mixed-up sort of life, and no experience of that life—not even when an American colonel almost had me shot as a German spy after I had parachuted behind the lines in France—has been more mixed up than the peculiar hell-to-heaven-to-purgatory existence I have had since I was first diagnosed as an acute leukemic. *In a way, no experience has been more interesting than living in intermittent intimacy* with the gentleman W. C. Fields used to call "the man in the white night gown" and whom I have come to think of as Uncle Thanatos, and sometimes, when I have been feeling very sick, as dear old Uncle Thanatos. Death is, after all, the only universal experience except birth and although a sensible person hopes to put it off as long as possible, *it is, even in anticipation, an interesting experience.* [Alsop, 1973: 11, emphasis added]

One might expect a professional writer to take a professional writer's interest in "an interesting experience." Yet there is certainly no determinate relationship between occupation and a specific space decision. The popular novelist, Jacqueline Susann, for example, if the newspaper accounts published after her death are accurate, chose, in direct contrast to Alsop, to keep her dying very much at the margins of her life. She shared the fact of her cancer with very few persons, continued writing fiction even when very ill and apparently committed nothing to paper about her journey to extinction.

Population

By the dimension of population, I refer to the question of whether the actor chooses to play out the dying role alone or with others who are also playing it out. Given the proportion of persons who die in hospitals (see pp. 33–34, above), it seems likely that even those who would prefer to go the whole way alone are often forced into the company of the dying "at the end." With sufficient resources, however, one can achieve an almost perfectly solo route, as did the "lone eagle," Charles Lindbergh.

> Two years before [his death], when he was 70, Lindbergh learned during a preoperative examination that he had lymphoma, a fatal disease. With the aid of radiation therapy, he was able to travel extensively—including a visit to the Philippines to study the Stone Age Tassaday tribe on Mindanao and to promote preservation of the monkey-eating eagle. From time to time, Howell [his physician] wrote, Lindbergh returned to Maui. He helped clear a neglected grave yard beside a picturesque church built by Yankee missionaries, selected his gravesite and made legal arrangements for his burial. As the disease made greater inroads, Lindbergh was hospitalized for several months. In August, 1974, he telephoned Hana [Maui, Hawaii] from New York. "This is Charles Lindbergh," Howell quoted him. "I have had a conference with my doctors and they advise me that I have only a short time to live.
>
> Please find me a cottage or a cabin near the village. I am coming home to Maui." He made the 5,000-mile trip on a stretcher and "was elated for the first few days," Howell said. "His appetite improved.

His fluid intake was adequate. There were regular morning conferences with the ranch superintendent to give instructions and receive
reports on the progress of the construction of his grave and the building of his simple coffin. He planned his funeral service along with
his family and requested that people attend in their work clothes."
Howell reported that as Lindbergh's lungs filled he required oxygen
from time to time and codeine "as necessary. Finally, he lapsed into
a coma and died 12 hours later," the doctor said. ["Doctor Tells of
Lindbergh's End," *The Sacramento Union,* May 20, 1975: A9][14]

Conversely, one may choose to spend important segments of
one's dying time and share important aspects of one's dying
experiences with others who are going the same way. Dying
"hospices" make this possible as do dying self-help or therapy
groups that have formed in some hospitals and communities
(see part III).[15] The extent to which terminal wards and nursing homes facilitate or hinder "group passage" by the dying is
unknown, although the available literature certainly suggests
the latter.[16]

Knowledge

By knowledge, I refer to the degree to which information about
one's admission to the dying role is shared with others—the
dying, the living, or both. One might conceive of the possibilities as a series of outwardly extending circles or zones. In the
minimal situation—the small center circle—only the M.D. and
the involved actor "know." In the maximal situation—the fur-
thest and largest circle—the whole world or at least everyone in
one's social order has access to the information.

The minimal knowledge situation is, by definition, impossible for an outsider to "know" about. The actor chooses, as it
were, to "pass," encountering all the advantages of being one of
the "living" and all the problems of information management

that Goffman has analyzed so well in *Stigma* (1963). An anonymous writer to Ann Landers provides one explanation for why one might choose the passing option.

> Dear Ann Landers: This may be one of the most unusual letters you have ever received. You see, I am dying. But don't become alarmed, and please don't feel sorry for me.
>
> After all, we are ALL dying. From the moment we are born we are headed toward inescapable death.
>
> Three years ago I learned I have chronic leukemia (I was 31, then). The doctor told me the truth at once because I insisted on knowing. The news came at a crisis time in my life. (I had just gone through a divorce and had young children to raise.)
>
> Would you believe I had to move out of town to a larger city because people would not accept me as a normal person? I was devastated, not by the disease, which has been controlled by drugs, but by the way I was treated. ... After I moved to this distant city my life changed dramatically. No one here knows of my illness and I am keeping my mouth shut. I work part-time, attend college, have many friends, and am involved with community activities and participate in sports. What a pity that I had to move to a town where nobody knew me in order to live a normal life.
>
> Although I feel well, look fine, and am managing beautifully, I know it can't last forever. I dread the day my friends must be told of my illness. I don't want to be pitied. And of course I fear that I may be deserted as I was once before. [Ann Landers, *Sacramento Union*, May 12, 1975]

It is interesting to note the degree to which "passing" closes off options on other dimensions. The life space devoted to dying must be minimal, one must be alone, and while a kind of dying stance (see below) is being expressed, no one but the actor herself or himself can appreciate it for what it is.

The minimal situation or its approximation has formed the plot of many a "tear-jerker" play, novel, and film. *Camille* is a classic example. *No Sad Songs for Me,* a 1950 American film, is one of the more affective of the modern versions. But I suspect that the number of dying persons who actually choose not to tell—who play out their dying in the manner of fictional melodrama—is really quite small. I would suspect, rather, that most people who must confront their own prolonged dying choose to share that confrontation with, at least, a select group of intimates.

The maximal situation is also an option, or at least it is so to the degree that one can secure access to the media. In the early and mid-1970s in America, that access would appear to have been remarkably easy, not simply for the already famous, like Stewart Alsop, who announced his admission to the dying category in his *Newsweek* column, but also for "ordinary" people whose only claim to distinction and attention was the fact that they had entered the dying role. This ease of access is, of course, a function of media gate-keepers' judgments relative to interest and saturation, and those judgments may vary through time. But when ease of access occurs, it provides the watching public with a continuous parade of dying models.

For the actors involved, one of the advantages of what I will call "media dying," is that one's opinions, feelings, observations, philosophies, and so forth are both elicited and, at least at some level, taken seriously. For most humans, that is not a common experience. Ted Rosenthal, the poet, who recorded his dying in both book and film *(How Could I Not Be among You,* 1973), and Stewart Alsop were persons who had an audience before they "became" dying. But Chuck McCracken, who chose to unplug himself from his kidney dialysis machine and died 81 days later, would not, in the ordinary course of events, have been asked to write his "own story" for the *National Enquirer.* It is as a dying person that Lois Jaffe, a social worker from Butler, Pennsylvania is given the opportunity to tell how she "copes" through an UPI reporter. Della Kilkenny would not have had the opportunity to tell a reporter "how lucky" she felt had she not been dying of cancer. Sharon Baptista's impending death from brain cancer received full page attention in the *Sacramento Bee;* Nancy Robinson was called "indomitable" by the *Los Angeles Times.* Delmar Stuermer had the opportunity to express both his anger at his emphysema and his desire to die to the readers of the *San Francisco Sunday Examiner and Chronicle* because he was dying. Ruth Howard's crusade for homemaker insurance was publicized by *Newsday* because she too was dying.[17] And so on for multitudes of ordinary people. Media dying allows some otherwise obscure persons a moment in the spotlight.

Media dying also increases the possibility that conflicts over style or over one or another dimension of style will emerge. I was told by an informant, for example, of an individual who was "kicked out of" his dying self-help group because he chose to allow a cinema verité film to be made of his dying passage and the group disapproved of media death. While speaking ill of the dead may eternally be considered "bad form" by many persons, speaking ill of those en route to death seems an inevitable concomitant of media dying.

Stance

By stance, I refer to something more elusive than the three dimensions outlined above. I refer to the character of emotional tone or orientation or personal philosophy that is expressed in the role.[18] Prolonged dying allows persons not only to act in certain ways vis-à-vis their dying but also to color their actions, to provide mood to their "being," to add demeanor to their doing.

Compare, for example, the "tone" conveyed by Ruth Hoffman with that expressed by Margorie Berg.

> Mrs. Hoffman, 57, was the cheerful hostess at the party she gave in her hospital room Saturday because—dying of bone cancer—she was afraid she might not last the weekend. ... "Everybody says I look better. Do you know why?" She pointed above her head toward the ceiling.
>
> "I have a date up there with God. Today is my happy day." [*Davis Enterprise*, August 13, 1973]
>
> She [Margorie Berg] says her doctor says she has "anywhere from a few months to several years" to live but that death can't come too soon for her. "Dying is really very boring," she says. [*Sacramento Bee*, April 2, 1975]

Hoffman is certainly a "jolly departer." Berg is merely "bored." Newspaper and other popular accounts of the dying process are rich mines of such diversity in demeanor—yielding up, as examples, the "brave reformer" (e.g., Greenfield, 1976), the "bemused and detached observer," the "serene and fatalistic acceptor," the "angry rebel," the "humanistic emoter," and so on. The variety of stance types is probably as large as human inventiveness can make it. My intent here is not to attempt an exhaustive cataloging of types, but rather to point up this important dimension of choice in the creation of the dying role.

Managing the Role: The Problem of Control

In the above, I have been emphasizing choice. I have been writing as if all dying persons are free to construct a dying *persona* in whatever way they wish. Of course this is not true. Even those who choose to "pass" are constrained by that decision and if they become too ill, the passing strategy will no longer be available to them. Lindbergh could opt to enact the role "solo" to the degree that he managed it because, as we saw, he had the requisite financial resources. For large numbers of the dying, that would simply not be an option. Conversely, a person might very much wish to share his dying with other dying but have no access to such persons. Space decisions, too, are hemmed in by circumstance. Some persons may be unable to devote much attention to their dying—because they have to go on working as long as they can, for example—even though they might wish the role to be central. Or, if one is extremely ill, a decision to relegate one's dying to the mere edges of one's focus and concern may easily crumble before the exigencies of pain and bodily needs. And under some circumstances, even stance may not withstand blockages to its expression.

> Besides the Lord Jim-Cyrano de Bergerac way of facing death, Thurber had always admired the dog's manner of dying, almost as much as its manner of living. In 1955, he wrote, in a piece about his poodle: "I know now and knew then, that no dog is fond of dying, but I have never had a dog that showed a human, jittery fear of death, either. Death, to a dog, is the final, unavoidable compulsion, the last ineluctable scent on a fearsome trail, but they like to face it alone, going out into the woods, among the leaves, if there are any leaves when their time comes, enduring without sentimental human distraction the Last Loneliness, which they are wise enough to know cannot be shared by anyone." But the quintessentially human James Thurber would not die in solitary majesty. He would be pummelled and punctured by doctors and nurses. [Bernstein, 1975: 501–502]

As with living roles, then, the creation of one's dying is both subject to choice and constrained by circumstance, by social organization, and by other human beings. Consider, for example, the sanctions visited upon this dying man because kin disapproved of his "style," as described in a letter to the Helen Bottel column.

Dear Helen: My uncle was a quiet, clean-minded, almost esthetic [sic] man who never swore when women were present and appeared never to have sexy thoughts.

At 68, he suffered a stroke and was paralyzed, but his mind seemed okay. He hasn't long, doctors say, as other complications have appeared.

But in these last months he has embarrassed his family terribly. He talks of nothing but women. He's apparently obsessed with sex.

His children tell people not to visit him at the hospital, and they don't come around much themselves. His wife leaves his room in tears. Easily shocked, she told me she didn't know he even knew these kinds of words.

How can dying change a man this much? [Bottel, 1976, emphasis added][19]

While dying, one may be freer at some times than at others. Persons in some locations may have more options in shaping their roles than persons in others.[20] But undoubtedly, for most who confront the dying role, part of the problem of construction is control.[21]

Available materials do not permit a fully developed analysis of this important aspect of role construction. But we can, I think, gain some appreciation of the exigencies of control by examining three "dyings" and by making comparisons among them relative to the operation and consequences of four "externals": (1) the disease process, (2) the social organization and culture of medical practice, (3) available resources, and (4) surrounding others. Let us consider, then, the dying experiences—as these experiences have been captured in print—of Charles "Wert" Wertenbaker, Edgar Snow and "Mrs. Abel."[22]

The dying of Charles Wertenbaker is surely one of the most graphically portrayed "trajectories" (Glaser and Strauss, 1968) in non-fictional literature. In a book published in 1957, Lael Wertenbaker, his spouse, chronicled this *Death of a Man* from the diagnosis of Wertenbaker's cancer in late September, 1954 through his suicide in early January 1955. As the author makes clear, Wertenbaker possessed a relatively well-developed and articulated conception of how he wished to die. Utilizing the dimensions of choice in role shaping discussed above, it is possible to summarize his "ideal" as involving marginal space, a solo route, a sharing of knowledge with a minimal number of friends and intimates and a stance that is perhaps best characterized as "Hemingway macho." "What he rejected, growing irascible at the thought of how often this was made possible in our age of medical miracles, was to live on *crippled* and *incomplete,* learning the ways and demands of living at any price, dependent on others, being less than himself, *less than a whole man*" (Wertenbaker, 1957: 46, emphasis added). As we shall see, to a significant degree, Wertenbaker "managed" to achieve the dying he wished, but he did so under less than auspicious conditions and the price of control was considerable struggle.

The dying of Edgar Snow—journalist and sympathetic historian of the Chinese Revolution—was also chronicled by his spouse, Lois Wheeler Snow, in her book *A Death with Dignity: When the Chinese Came,* published in 1974. The period covered is shorter than in Wertenbaker's case—from late November, 1971 when the discovery of an enlarged liver led to a diagnosis of carcinoma of the pancreas and surgery, until February 15, 1972 when he died—and that shorter period is less graphically portrayed. Snow viewed his dying more obliquely than did Wertenbaker, he sidled toward self-knowledge rather than walking to it directly and there is little evidence that he pronounced any well-articulated "dying philosophy." From his behavior before and after the diagnosis, however, one might presume that had he had the opportunity, he would have kept his dying very much at the margins of his life, sharing his knowledge with minimal or no others. But as I shall describe in a moment, he did not have the opportunity to enact those choices. He was enabled, however, by a truly incredible set of events, to die solo and with a stance of "serene quietness," despite routine circumstances that would normally have precluded the expression of these role preferences.

In the case of Mrs. Abel (a pseudonym), it is difficult to speak of role construction or dimensions of choice at all. As her dying is portrayed by sociologists Anselm Strauss and Barney Glaser in *Anguish: A Case History of a Dying Trajectory* (1970), it seems most accurately characterized by the absence of control—seemingly because it was consumed by a struggle for control. From her first hospital admission in late August or September for treatment of breast cancer until her death the following February, the "externals" of Mrs. Abel's dying—her death milieu, as it were-wrapped her in a strait jacket of others' actions, others' beliefs, others' preferences. To understand more clearly what happened to Mrs. Abel as well as to Wertenbaker and Snow, we shall view their dying experiences in terms of four crucially important "externals," beginning with the disease process itself.

The Disease Process

As indicated above, Charles Wertenbaker's ideal included the containment of his dying at the margins of his life. He wanted "good time": to write, to swim, to make love, to be with his children, to go on living "as a man," until the end came. He didn't quite manage it. When cancer was first diagnosed, he and Lael were living in a small village on the coast of France. They returned to the U.S. where surgery made clear there was "nothing to be done." They then decided to return to their village, but rather than fly, they would go by boat for a last holiday. There was no holiday. Instead, they spent the boat trip coping—unaided by medical expertise—with a painful and almost fatal abscess. And while there were occasional periods after they returned to their village when life was "almost normal," more and more time—night and day—was consumed by the necessity to cater to the disease itself, to pain, and to pain control. Eventually, and sooner than anticipated, the amount of time and energy consumed by dying reached an unacceptable level.

> On the 7th, by the fire, he said: "That's the last time I can make those stairs. I can't hear music any more. I can't drink even tea. The cigarettes taste bad. I'm only staying alive to see your face."
>
> It had to be that night, if it was to be his way, and we both knew it. We waited until very late, talking together with a kind of final serenity unmatched at any other time. He planned everything most carefully, aware that nothing was as you planned it, but with determination that however and whatever, he must die. Debating the amount in case it should make him too shaky, he took a small last shot of morphine. I brought his Rolls razor, freshly stropped, and he detached the blade. [Wertenbaker, 1957: 180]

Like Wertenbaker, Edgar Snow—if we may read between the lines of his actions—would have preferred to keep his dying marginal. Like Wertenbaker, too, he was unable to do so. From late November through late December, the days were consumed with surgery and with the recovery from surgery and with the physical-focusing demands of hospital life. And even after his return home, pain, weakness, illness forced his dying into a central position in his life space.

> Nudging our way through cotton-white fog on the iciest night of the year, I drove Ed home. The plate-glass hospital doors had, swung shut; with their closing, surgeons and specialists became shadow

people to be contacted at office hours through remote secretaries or recorded messages. Our neighborhood doctors took over, in touch with the original team, but that was of little meaning at three o'clock in the morning when the day's pills were finished and interminable hours stretched ahead before the next prescribed allotment. ... Daytime was better. Light reduced the night terror, brought a semblance of normality, allowed us energy to move around our broken health. ... When a pallid January sun became enticing, I'd walk to the village and back with Ed, an obvious strain for him, this outing, but a need nevertheless, a pinning of himself to normal activity. He had always walked to the village. ... An evening came when Ed felt well enough to dine downstairs. Chris and Sian [Snow children] opted for a rare night out, seeing us first comfortable in the living room with music and cocktails in front of the fire. Ed sat in the "new" chair—one I had admired in a Geneva store window with him and he'd gone back to buy for my birthday in July. It's striped in Scandinavian orange and rust against a wheaten white; the colors match the room, alive with books in the wall-wide shelves Ed had carefully measured, cut, placed and polished. He wore his Christmas pajamas and robe, I a long wool skirt. The decorated tree was still up. ... Light flickered from the candles on the coffee table between us; we talked about books, the children, the leak in the roof, while Joan Baez's silver voice filled in the pauses. I see us there each time I enter the room, now that it's all past, because at that moment, then, in isolated ease, it seemed the way it had always been—until Ed shook his head "no" to dessert, looking suddenly shattered, and I helped him up to bed. He could hardly crawl in. That night promised to be rough; there was only one permitted pill left until morning. [Snow, 1974: 70–72]

In Mrs. Abel's case, the degree to which the disease process interfered with role construction choices is unclear primarily because the other externals of her dying conspired to muffle the expression—even verbal expression—of choice. Relative to one aspect of the workings of her cancer on her body, however, Mrs. Abel's preferences were clear. She wanted to minimize if not totally eliminate her perceived pain. She was not very successful in this regard but again, because of the way in which other factors operated, it is difficult to ascertain the degree to which this failure was a function of the disease itself. Intruding upon her dying, as well as upon the dyings of the others, were the social organization and culture of medical practice.

The Social Organization and Culture of Medical Practice

For Mrs. Abel, for Edgar Snow and for Charles Wertenbaker, the practices and beliefs of the surrounding and dominant medical milieux did not mesh with their own desires. Wertenbaker, for example, wished to know the truth about his condition, his physicians wished to "spare" him. He wanted to go on living only if the living were "good enough." Medical practice demanded that every effort be made to prolong his life to the utmost, even if hospitalization and repeated surgery were the costs. He wished to protect himself from what he viewed as the degrading consequences of constant pain. Medical ethics were concerned with the risk of addiction. He demanded the right to choose the time of his demise. His French physician could view such a possibility only with horror.

> "When he wants to die, he can do that, too," I [Lael Wertenbaker] said.
>   "You can't let him kill himself!" said Cartier. "You cannot."
>   "Why not?"
>   "You would not kill him?"
>   "No! And I don't want him to die one day sooner, God knows, but do you understand me, it's up to *him* what he does!"
>   "You would help him do that!" he said in horrified comprehension. "I believe you would. This is serious. *You must not.*" [Wertenbaker, 1957: 144]

In contrast to Wertenbaker, Snow apparently did not want the "hard truth." He preferred a more gradual and oblique approach to his mortality. He got the hard truth anyway.

> As he [a surgeon] gave me his report (bad), something made me realize it must be a repetition of what he had said inside [Snow's hospital] room.
> "You didn't tell this to my husband?"
> "But of course, madame. Why not?"
> "It ... was *understood* you were to discuss this with me first!"
> He blinked, uncertain. "You are Americans. It is well known that in your country the patient is always told." [Snow, 1974: 62]

Also unlike Wertenbaker, Snow was willing to prolong his dying through weakness and total dependence. His own apparently preferred stance of serene quietness was not violated by any conceptions of "being less than a whole man." But like Wertenbaker, he too wished to be spared the degrading and stance-interfering consequences of constant pain.

And like Wertenbaker, he was surrounded by medical beliefs and practices that ordained that pain control was important but only if it could be achieved without risk of addiction or shortening of life. "We were given a packet of pills, painkillers and sedatives, to be used sparingly: don't overdo! Ed's liver, the body's filter, was so far gone that a "normal" amount of drugs risked creating a hepatic coma. I had no idea of the forthcoming nights when the whole packet could not have stopped the pain or induced sleep" (Snow, 1974: 70).

For Mrs. Abel, the *struggle* for pain control consumed her dying experience. Whatever other choices she might have made relative to her dying were never expressed because her time and energy were devoted to the continuing battle with a dominating and surrounding medical world over the issue of her pain. Both

Wertenbaker and Snow spent *some* of their dying time in the midst of the medical world's total institution—the hospital; Mrs. Abel spent *most* of her time there. And her perception of her suffering and what should be done about it differed radically from the perceptions of her keepers.

Mrs. Abel spent quite a bit of time weeping off and on, telling about [her past]. Also she said the nurses didn't come in to see her very often: she frequently put on her buzzer, but no one would come. When I [the researcher] went out to have the nurses tell me about this patient, they told me she [Mrs. Abel] kept a notebook: every time she had medication, she would jot down in her notebook what she had had—the kind of medication, the timing, and whether it was an injection or pill. She was getting both. At that time she was on methadone, percodan, and darvon. She would alternate them. She had a schedule she regulated so as to get something every hour for pain. When one nurse told me this, I realized she was rather annoyed about this. There were frequent notes in the cardex in these first two or three weeks about Mrs. Abel wanting her pain medications around the clock. Finally, Dr. Colp wrote orders that she could have the medications. But the nurses didn't want to wake her up at night. Then Mrs. Abel got to setting an alarm clock so she could wake up to receive pain medication. This, of course, never goes over very well with a group of nurses who feel you should not wake up patients to give pain medication: if they're sleeping through all this, then they don't have pain! Mrs. Abel's explanation was that if she waited until morning to get the medication, the pain got such a start that the medication then didn't take care of the pain.[23] She wanted a consistent dosage of medication; she was very frightened of pain. The nurses said the first thing in the morning—6:30—Mrs. Abel was on the buzzer for her medication. This was a real problem to them. They were annoyed, they were irritated, and they were complaining among themselves. ... During this early two-week period, the next thing was that the nurses stated, "She is on the buzzer all the time." ... but the patient told me that the nurses "keep holding off." The girls [sic] described this tactic as "We try and get her to hold off for at least two hours between medications." [Strauss & Glaser, 1970: 34–35]

Available Resources

Despite the rapid progress of their diseases and despite the medical milieux that surrounded them, both Wertenbaker and Snow managed, to a significant degree, to control the shape of their dyings. They did so in part because they commanded sufficient resources. Some of these were *financial*. The Wertenbakers for example, while by no means wealthy, did not require "charity ward" care for Wert, they could afford to travel to the U.S. for surgery and then return to France, they had funds to pay for requisite drugs, and the economics of life in their small village made possible a house-keeper and other service personnel that bought them the time to devote to "Wert's" dying management. Lois and Edgar Snow were not wealthy either, but by any standards, they were affluent. They lived in a village in Switzerland not far from Geneva and despite problems with the hospital care they received,

> they were about the best conditions one could *buy* anywhere in the United States or Western Europe. A private Swiss clinic provides external comforts and modern facilities that must rate as luxurious in comparison to many Western equivalents: one can purchase amenities and physical decencies that blunt the sharp rupture of normal life forced into hospital restriction and at a far lesser cost than in the United States. Even for a foreigner the toll, including room service, phone, etc., for Ed's stay in private room with bath, was a fraction of the price it would have been at home. [Snow, 1974: 52]

Other of the available resources were in *"connections."* Both the Wertenbakers were writers. Wert had been for many years an editor for Time, Inc. They were acquainted with important segments of the educated elite in both Europe and the United States. They knew people "who knew people." These connections enabled them to choose their medical attendants from among friends, to live in rent-free comfort while Wert was recovering from surgery, to get first-class accommodations on a fully booked ship and, most importantly, to secure legally and illegally the drugs they needed to keep Wert's pain under control. The Snows had connections too. In addition to American and European friends who had the resources and time to make the trip to their Swiss village to provide assistance and comfort, they also had Chinese friends, among them, Mao Tse-tung and Chou En-lai. And those connections, as we shall see, created for Edgar Snow a dying that came close to being the one he wished.

In stark contrast, Mrs. Abel had no personal resources, either financial or "in connections." She could not afford private hospitalization or sustained private medical care. Her dying was located in a state-operated, medical-school-linked "teaching hospital" rather than in a county hospital only because she was initially a participant in medical research. She knew no one who was "anyone" or who could help her battle the medical world in which she was so thoroughly enmeshed. In fact, she was entirely without that which both Wertenbaker and Snow had in such crucial abundance: supportive surrounding others. ·

Surrounding Others

In the case of Wertenbaker, I think it is accurate to say that he was finally and most crucially enabled to shape his dying to the degree he did (1) because potentially influential opponents to that shaping were *not present,* and (2) because he had in Lael Wertenbaker an *ally* who believed implicitly in what he wanted to do and who did everything she could to realize his desires. By returning to France after the surgery, the Wertenbakers put distance between themselves and those close family and friends who might have disagreed and interfered with the course on which they embarked. Many of these did not know that "dying" had begun; even those who did were unaware—because they were not present to monitor—just how drugs were being secured and used, just what sorts of decisions were being made about proffered surgery, or that there was no question of waiting for the end to come "naturally." In their relative isolation from on-the-spot surveillance, then, the Wertenbakers gained considerable freedom to control. But it was Lael Wertenbaker who enabled that control to be exercised. It was she who insisted that Wert's wishes be honored and that he be told the "truth," despite accusations from physicians that in her demands she was expressing not honesty but cruelty. It was she who handled the "telling" to friends and family that allowed the minimal knowledge sharing that Wert desired. It was she who, conquering her aversion to sickness and physical distress, mopped up after out-of-control bowels and draining abscesses, gave shots for pain and sat up through the repeated *"crises"* to provide the nursing care that enabled Wertenbaker to do his dying "solo" and at home. And it was she who battled with their French physician over Wert's refusal to undergo a surgery (involving a colostomy) that might have prolonged his life but that would have degraded him in his own eyes and undercut his preferred stance towards dying. Given the rapid progress of his disease and the hostility of the medical milieu, only an ally as strong, faithful, and devoted as his spouse would have or could have used their available resources to buy Wertenbaker the dying he desired.

For Edgar Snow, the absence of potential opponents *to his dying style* did not have the import it had for Wertenbaker, primarily because his rather covertly expressed dying preferences did not involve beliefs or actions that influential others were likely to find controversial. Nonetheless, the fact that his dying was located in Switzerland rather than in the United States and the consequent absence of what might be viewed as broadly political opponents, was crucial. For this Swiss location made possible and unproblematic the presence in the Snow home of a set of pivotally important supportive others: a medical team from the Republic of China.

> When Hans came down from his talk with Ed, I showed him the special-delivery letter which had just arrived. Peking had acted: Mao Tse-tung and Chou En-lai were sending a medical team of doctors and nurses. They wanted to escort us all back to China. [Snow, 1974: 79]
>
> They came as friends as well as experts, these Chinese citizens; they came with undivided commitment. They saw at once the inroads of the dreadful disease and they knew the trip to Peking was no longer feasible. The evening after they arrived Shag said, "We had made a home out of a hospital for you in Peking; now we'll stay here and make a hospital out of your home." And this they did, with expertise, patience and devotion, making it possible for their American friend to spend his last weeks with his family in relative peace and calm. Without them this would not have been achieved, and a return to routinized hospitalization would have been inevitable. Through them, home and hospital blended. ... They were able not only to release him from the worst of his physical misery but to bring him a tranquility, a dignity in dying that made it more bearable—not only for him but for me, for our two children, and for our families and friends. [Snow, 1974: 95–96]

The progress of Snow's disease forced his dying into the center of his life when he would have preferred it at the margins. For the same reason, knowledge of his dying was much more widely shared that he undoubtedly would have wished. But because of the presence of a Chinese medical team, he was enabled—as he would otherwise not have been, given routine medical practice and belief—to realize the desire to die "solo" and with a stance of serene quietness.

For Mrs. Abel, there were no allies, only opponents. Her spouse rarely visited her at the hospital and in no meaningful sense could he be said to have participated in her dying. She was essentially friendless. Her dying ended as it had proceeded: surrounded by hostile others, characterized by helplessness, marked by the absence of a self-created dying identity.

> The most vital force shaping the end of Mrs. Abel's dying trajectory was the growing *intolerance* of the staff to her complaints of pain, her ritualistic demands during baths, meals, pain medication, and so forth and her abiding need for companionship and attention which were further stimulated by the staffs avoidance of her. ... There were three major consequences of this intolerance for Mrs. Abel's last days. The first was the pressure the nursing staff put on Dr. Colp to *discharge* her. ... The second was the growing *isolation* of Mrs. Abel. Again this reduced the calibre of her care. A third consequence was that the staff did not help Mrs. Abel *prepare* herself for death on a daily basis. [Strauss and Glaser, 1970: 165]

In the foregoing, we have been considering the efforts of individual actors to construct a dying role or identity—a construction effort necessitated for many contemporary humans by the increasingly prolonged period between admission to the category, dying, and extinction. But, as we have seen, there are limits to the freedom of the individual actor to shape the role as he or she may see fit, especially *if* that desired shaping does not conform to the exigencies of disease, medical practice, available resources, or surrounding others. Some persons, because of a lucky combination of elements in their dying situation, may find it relatively easy to achieve a preferred identity. Others, like Charles Wertenbaker or Edgar Snow, may approximate their ideal only with considerable struggle or with the benefit of extraordinary circumstances. Certainly the dying experiences of both Wertenbaker and Snow suggest that given the exigencies of disease processes and a medical milieu whose gamut of practices and beliefs are unlikely to coincide with everyone's preferences, most individuals will be able to have a hand in shaping their dyings only if they are abetted by sufficient available resources and by sympathetic and supportive surrounding others. For large numbers of humans, like Mrs. Abel, access to resources and others may be blocked. As such, their capacity to create the conditions that allow control will not easily be accomplished individually. More collective efforts may be needed. To such emerging collective efforts, we now turn.

III Collective Constructions: The Happy Death Movement

I have been arguing that an important component of the modern face of death is the prolongation of the dying period. Dying is now, as it has not been historically, something one can "be" long enough for that period of "being" to be viewed as problematic; long enough for the questions of how to act, what collectively to do and what it all means anyway to be raised. I have suggested that some portion of the activity surrounding death and dying that has been so apparent in more recent years is the activity of individual humans confronting this new potential for shaping a role and shaping it. Most such *individual* activity, however, undoubtedly occurs out of view. The major portion of the publicly visible death doings is rather, I would judge, the product of more *collective* efforts and concerns. In this part, we shall be exploring a complex set of emergent actions, groups, and beliefs that are usefully analyzed as a collectivity—a social movement.[1] I shall refer to this collectivity as the "happy death movement."[2]

In the previous pages, we were concerned with individual role construction activities as they addressed themselves to one of the questions raised by the situation of modern dying: "how shall I act?" Here, we shall be concerned with the happy death movement in terms of its developing answers to the two other questions: "what shall we do?" and "what does it mean?" We shall, that is, focus on two aspects of the movement: its activities relative to structural reform and its creation of ideology. Before turning to these matters, however, I want first to give the reader a brief idea of the character of the groups, activities, and persons that form the phenomena here under scrutiny.

The collectivity that I am calling the "happy death movement" is a sprawling, diverse, multi-structured, diffuse assemblage of persons, acting independently and as parts of organizations, engaging in a multiplicity of largely uncoordinated activities and possessing varying degrees of "consciousness" relative to their participation in a movement. It is in fact, in many ways, closer to what Blumer calls a *general social movement*—characterized by groping, uncoordinated efforts, lacking established leadership and recognizable membership and with a literature as varied and ill-defined as the movement itself—than to a *specific social movement* with its recognized and accepted leadership, definite membership, and articulate "culture" (Blumer, 1969a: 10–11; see also Wilson, 1973: 11–13). On the other hand, there would also appear to be enough of a leadership, enough of a we-consciousness, enough coordination and so on, at least at some levels, to make it a less than ideal example of a general social movement. Rather, like the contemporary women's movement, the happy death movement would seem to be a mixed type. Look here and one sees diffuseness, lack of articulate organization and a set of people acting relatively independently. Look elsewhere and one sees coordination, membership, leaders, focused goals.

While one may certainly argue over the appropriate "type" classification for the phenomena at issue here, there is little question I think but that they are generally best conceived in social movement terms. Whether one uses Blumer's very terse definition:

collective enterprises to establish a new order of life [1969a: 8]

or Turner and Killian's more detailed

collectivity acting with some continuity to promote or resist a change in the society or group of which it is a part. As a collectivity a movement is a group with indefinite and shifting membership and with leadership whose position is determined more by the informal response of the members than by formal procedures for legitimizing authority [1972: 246],

the phenomena that are the happy death movement are well captured.

More specifically, the individuals, organizations, and activities that are the movement are concerned with promoting a change in American society with regard to its beliefs about death and dying, its emotional responses to death and dying, and its legal and normative practices relative to death and dying. They are attempting, that is, to "establish a new order of life" relative to death. Numerous of these change proponents are intellectuals, unconnected to any particular group or organization but promoting change through lectures, books, courses, and so forth. Other change proponents are organized into such diverse entities as the Euthanasia Educational Council, the Foundation of Thanatology, Ars Moriendi, the Forum for Death Education and Counselling, Shanti, Threshold, Inc., Bereavement Outreach, the Widow-to-Widow Program, Hospice of Marin, California and Hospice, Inc., of New Haven, Connecticut, Compassionate Friends and innumerable named and unnamed patient, patient and family, or family self-help groups. Participants—organizationally affiliated or otherwise—seem, to the degree

that this can be judged,[3] generally to be white, relatively affluent, both "straight" and counterculture in style, and, unsurprisingly, heavily representative of such occupations as physician,
nurse, clergyman, social worker, psychiatrist, psychologist, and
counsellor. Participation by the dying or their immediate families seems quite variable. In some groups—self-help groups for
example—only the dying may be involved. Other groups—the
Forum for Death Education and Counselling, for example—are
primarily composed of medical, counselling, or education "professionals." As relationships to the movement, organizations
within the movement, and members of the movement vary, so
do the means or mechanisms by which change is attempted:
books, films, newsletters, lobbying efforts, creation of new medical organizations, lectures, courses, conferences,[4] journals, and
counselling.

In attempting, then, to "capture" some truths about this
assemblage, one confronts the distortion-creating fact that the
"thing" one wishes to speak about is *many things*. Additionally,
the thing—in its multiplicity—is emergent in the mid and late
seventies. It is *in the process of being created*. One tries to pin down
with the static point of the written word that which is fluid. I ask
the reader to bear these provisos in mind as we proceed.

What Shall We Do? Structural Reform

Out of the diverse activities of the happy death movement,[5] certain patterns have emerged that may be understood as providing answers to one of the questions raised by the situation of
modern dying—"what shall we do?" Given the increasing numbers of people who are taking so long to die in a bureaucratic
and secular world, what shall we do about it? One possible and

logical answer, of course, is "nothing." Just let things go as they are. But social movements do not arise in order to advocate the status quo. They arise, presumably, out of some persons' felt dissatisfaction with what they perceive as what is and, therefore, movements concern themselves not with maintenance but with change—which change is defined by participants as "reform." For the happy death movement, then, what we should *do* relative to the situation of modern death and dying is *talk about it, rearrange it* and *legislate it.*

Talk about It

The assertion that death is or has been until the mid-seventies a taboo topic in America and that such a taboo is bad is, as we shall see, a cornerstone of one aspect of the happy death movement's emergent ideology. It is not surprising, then, that an important focus of reform activities is the destruction of this presumed "structure of silence." In my view (see L. Lofland, 1976), there is considerable question about the amount of death talk that may have occurred at the private level prior to the birth of movement efforts. But there is little question that the amount of public and *organized* talk about death greatly increased in the U.S. during the mid-1960 to mid-1970 period. In truth, in some important senses, the movement is "talk." Great quantities of its "doings" involve talking—"therapeutically" and "educationally"—about dying, about death: other people's, one's own, in the present, in the future.

Death Talk as Therapy

A crucial component of much of this talkativeness is defined as "grief therapy." The presumed *need* for such therapy is linked to the general acceptance by movement participants and sympathizers of what we may conceive as the "conventional perspective on grief." This perspective holds that grief is a universal human emotion or set of emotions, generally triggered by any loss the actor finds significant. It has an internally generated "normal course" (it is a *process)* that, for the health of the actor, must be "worked through." Anything which blocks the beginning of the process in the first place or that interrupts or stalls its progression is negative and results in "pathological" or "abnormal" grief reactions.[6] For example:

> According to [Dr. David] Peretz … delayed or inhibited grief is unhealthy. Lingering depression. Immersing oneself in work to block feeling. Persistent chronic mourning represents denial of the reality of the loss. … Susan Sherman and Joan Rolsky at St. Christopher's [in Philadelphia] think, "It's abnormal to grieve and not let anyone in. It's not healthy to keep a dead person alive in the form of a shrine. Like leaving the room untouched. You've got to work out your relationship to the deceased and be able to form new relationships. That's why we start to worry if they're still withdrawn after six months. [Kron, 1973]

Talking as "therapy", then, is said to help one *get through* the grief process, removing any blockages and either curing or averting any pathologies.

Opportunities for doing "therapeutic" death talk vary considerably in form. Numerous groups like Compassionate Friends, an organization of parents who have experienced the death of a child, follow the Alcoholics Anonymous or Recovery, Inc., model, doing their talking only with others who have shared their experience.

> Each meeting opens with an affirmation of personal tragedies in the style of Alcoholics Anonymous: "My name is Ernie Freireich, and I am a bereaved parent. I lost my son Mark in an automobile accident." Each lasts as long as members want to air feelings and think they can provide mutual support.

Only in such a setting, explains Freireich, whose 16-year-old son was killed two years ago, "do you feel able to talk freely with another person who's been down the same street you've been down, without having judgment passed on you." Knowing that their listeners understand, the participants feel free to express the depths of their pain and bitterness. [Seligmann, with Agrest, 1977; see also Silverman, 1976 on the Widow-to-Widow program]

In some communities, telephone "hot lines" for the dying and the families of the dying have been established, usually staffed by volunteers. More importantly, at least from the point of view of opportunities for professional employment, is the growth of "death" counselling as an occupational specialty.[7] Increasing numbers of therapists and counsellors—psychologists, psychiatrists, ministers, priests, and rabbis, for example—have either added "grief work," "therapy for the dying," "therapy for the bereaved" or some such to their repertoire of other services, or devote themselves exclusively to this concern. (See Wood, 1976b, 1977; Kerr, 1974; Kron, 1973, 1975.) And for those who prefer to do their therapeutic death talk with themselves, innumerable "how to" books are available, including such titles as *Grief and How to Live with It* (Morris, 1972); *How to Survive the Loss of a Love* (Colgrove, Bloomfield and McWilliams, 1976) and *Death's Single Privacy: Grieving and Personal Growth* (Phipps, 1974).

Death Talk as Education

At any given moment, the audience for therapeutic death talk is necessarily limited. A more wide-ranging effort to break the alleged structure of silence involves "death education"—with a target population no less than that of the entire nation state. Through a multiplicity of locales and ages, American humans are to be taught to stop avoiding death and to "accept it" both intellectually and emotionally.

> When you die, you're dead. Try saying that word, DEAD. It is a hard word to say, isn't it? Not hard to pronounce, really, but hard to make yourself say. Maybe because it's a sad word ... even a little frightening. Let's say it again: DEAD. Now, let's say another word: DIE. That's what happened to grandfather. Grandfather died. He is dead. It is not like playing cowboys and Indians. "BANG! I shot you. You are dead!" And then you start all over again and play another game. DEAD IS DEAD. It is not a game. It is very real. Grandfather is gone. He will never come back. [Grollman, ed., 1970: 8–9]

This extract is from a book that attempts to help parents teach their pre-school children about death, but the message that it contains is very little different than the message being propounded in a host of grade-school courses, high-school courses, college courses and adult education courses; in regional and national workshops, symposia, and conferences; in community forums; and in countless books. Consider, for example, this newspaper description of a high-school-level death course:

> "The curtain of mystery about death is being rolled back. The subject is not something that should be swept under the rug," says a high school psychologist who has 150 students in classes about death. ... "If a student is uncomfortable with any topic, he is excused from the class and assigned other work. We have had only two or three drop out," Wellman said. "When the students come out of the courses they certainly look at life a little differently. The uncomfortable feelings we have when the subject of death comes up can be removed." ["High School Death Class Seeks to End Mystery," *Los Angeles Times*, November 17, 1976]

Or these accounts of college courses:

> People should face death and be deeply hurt by it because it is as much a part of life as birth, says a psychologist who teaches a course on coping with death. Douglas Michell, psychology professor at California State University at Sacramento, said Americans don't know how to deal with death because they avoid talking about it. "Face it,

feel the tragedy, be deeply hurt by it," Michell said he tells students in his course called "The Psychological Aspects of Death"—one of the most popular at the university. ... His students talk about their experiences with death to help remove the taboo on the subject. ... "We try to take away the negative element in death," said Michell. ["Students Forced to Face Death," *Sacramento Union,* July 20, 1977]

From his unique vantage point as an expert in both [sex and death), Leviton [a professor at the University of Maryland] asserts that "death has replaced sex as the taboo subject of our times." Consequently, he says, the purpose of "looking at death" in his course is to help students "lead happier lives." ["A Course on Death," *Newsweek,* May 8, 1972][8]

Or this commentary from a brochure promoting an Association for Humanistic Psychology sponsored conference on "The Art of Dying":

The denial of any significant part of ourselves, individually or in society, must be paid for in terrible ways: anxiety, depression, violence. AHP offers this program in the belief that open dialogue among thoughtful people can best help us explore these blocked and feared areas of our experience.

We have assembled a select group of these who work with the dying and the bereaved, who have written and done research on death and dying. We hope that it will help to reduce the fear of life— often expressed as fear and denial of death.

The art of living—dealing with our lives as important, unique, and with great potential for growth—will be enhanced when it is extended to include the *whole* of our experience. We celebrate the beginning of life; perhaps we can learn to celebrate its climax and learn the Art of Dying. [Basayne, 1974]

In these extracts, we get an early glimpse of some of the emergent themes of movement ideology—a matter we shall consider shortly. Here we need only note that much movement activity involves attempts to "educate" the populace about death.

Rearrange It

As we saw in part I, an important component of the modern face of death, of the situation of modern dying, is that it is bureaucratized. For many contemporary humans, goodly portions of their dying time is spent in hospitals, under the control of dominant medical practices and beliefs and regulated by the rationalized concerns of medical bureaucracies. In the main, movement proponents and sympathizers have not found these arrangements satisfactory.[9] They have argued—among many other complaints—that hospitals' emphasis on "cure" makes them poor settings for prolonged dying: that the needs of the dying are submerged to the routine of instrumental care; that hospital personnel are unable to deal emotionally with prolonged dying and that the dying thus becomes targets for personnel's fears and dislike; and that the focus on continuous treatment even in the face of inevitable death eventuates in disattention to the comfort of the dying person. As a consequence of such complaints, a second focus of reform activities within the happy death movement is the rearrangement of the structure of care for the dying.[10]

It is, of course, much easier to generate "talk" as a reform activity than to rearrange or reorganize societal institutions—as many a moribund social movement can testify. Understandably then, activity in this area is more effort than accomplishment.

As well as can be judged in the late seventies, rearrangement activity is primarily concerned with two oddly opposite but presumably complementary models of alternative care patterns. In the first, a special "dying place" is created—either as a separate organization or within an existing medical facility. In the dying place, the emphasis is on the "comfort," "serenity," and "happiness" of the dying person. No attempt is made to prolong life, the orientation of the staff is primarily affective not instrumental, and typically Western hospital rules are eschewed. The model requires that the environment be designed "from the patient's point of view, with an at-home feeling" (Kron, 1976).

The second pattern involves the creation of arrangements that will, obversely, desegregate dying, which will return it to the home. Here the model specifies that the ideal is the "home death," where the person is surrounded by familiar things, ensconced in the bosom of his or her family, comforted by the chance to die where he or she had lived. The mechanisms for the realization of this model are considerably more complex than for the creation of the dying place: insurance that pays for at-home care; the availability of housekeepers and medical and other support personnel who make house calls; the availability of home-use equipment for palliative care and so forth.

Both models are largely the creation of a single person: Cicely Saunders, a British physician and the founder of London's St. Christopher's Hospice.

> At St. Christopher's the unit of care is not just the patient but also the family; the place of care is the patient's home—where studies show most people would prefer to die—for as long as possible. In fact, St. Christopher's cheery 54-bed inpatient facility is actually a backup unit and patients often go back and forth between the hospice and home. [Kron, 1976: 43]

And the philosophy that infuses the models is, not exclusively, but certainly thoroughly Saunders's as well.

> To go on pressing for acute, active treatment at a stage when a patient has gone too far and should not be made to return is not good medicine. There is a difference between prolonging living and what can really only be called prolonged dying. Because something is possible does not mean that it is necessarily either right or kind to do it. One

often sees a great weariness with the sort of pain and illness that brings our patients to us such as that of Sir William Osler who, when he was dying, said, "I'm too far across the river now to want to come back and have it all over again." I do not think he would have given a "thank you" to someone who pulled him back at that stage. Recognition of this stage is not defeatism either on the part of the patient or on that of the doctor. Rather it is respect and awareness of the individual person and his dignity. When one patient came to us, she described her situation by saying, "It was *all* pain. ..." The treatment at St. Joseph's is designed to relieve the pain. Yes, one *can* do that, to enable the patient not only to die peacefully but to live fully until he dies, living as himself, neither swamped with distress nor smothered by treatments and drugs and the things that we are doing; nor yet enduring in sterile isolation. [Saunders, 1969: 52–53][11]

The attempt to import these models for dying care from their British birthplace to the North American continent has yet, as indicated above, been only minimally successful in terms of concrete arrangements.[12] There is certainly no question but that Saunders's message has been widely broadcast—verbally and in print—to the medical profession. But its long-term positive reception by that profession remains highly problematic.[13]

Legislate It

A third focus of movement activity involves attempts to alter the "structure of law" in such a way as to provide the individual actor with the power to make certain decisions about the type of medical care he or she will receive under "dying" conditions. In essence this has meant that actors should be granted the legal right to terminate efforts to prolong their lives. The mechanism advocated has been some form of a "living will"—one version of which has long been circulated by the Euthanasia Educational Council.

To My Family, My Physician, My Clergyman, My Lawyer:

If the time comes when I can no longer take part in decisions for my own future, let this statement stand as the testament of my wishes:

If there is no reasonable expectation of my recovery from physical or mental disability, I, _____, request that I be allowed to die and not be kept alive by artificial means or heroic measures. Death is as much a reality as birth, growth, maturity and old age—it is the one certainty. I do not fear death as much as I fear the indignity of deterioration, dependence and hopeless pain. I ask that medication be mercifully administered to me for terminal suffering even if it hasten the moment of death. This request is made after careful consideration. Although this document is not legally binding, you who care for me will, I hope, feel morally bound to follow its mandate. I recognize that it places a heavy burden or responsibility upon you, and it is with the intention of sharing that responsibility and of mitigating any feelings of guilt that this statement is made.

As with rearrangement activities, there has been more effort than accomplishment.[14] But the topic of concern, variously phrased as euthanasia, "death with dignity," or "natural death," has at least succeeded in garnering considerable media attention[15] and providing the focus for widespread debate.[16]

We have been reviewing some of the happy death movement's answers to the question of what to do in the face of modern death. But no movement limits itself only to pre-scribing action. All movements are concerned as well with prescribing belief. It is to the happy death movement's emergent prescriptions in that area that we now turn.

What Does It Mean? Emergent Ideology

Social movements, as I have said, are not merely the creators of activities or new organizational forms. They do not merely attempt to rearrange social furniture. They are also, importantly, creators of ideology, constructors of conceptions. The women's movement, for example, is not merely a mover behind divorce reform or the ERA attempt or the creation of child care facilities. It is also the creator or the synthesizer or the carrier of ideas about the proper relation between the sexes, about the appropriate meanings of male and female. The ecology movement is not merely a force that battles to enlarge parks or pass legislation involving the necessity for environmental impact reports. It is also the constructor of conceptions about the appropriate relationships between human beings and the planet earth, conceptions about the priority of certain long-term values over other shorter-term concerns. So, too, the happy death movement is not just concerned with hospices and euthanasia legislation and new therapeutic opportunities. It is profoundly involved as well with conceptions of the appropriate character and meaning of death and dying.

I want here to consider two fundamental aspects of the movement's complex and emergent ideology: the evocation of enemy and the developing articulation of some important belief components of a "dying craft." Before turning to these matters, however, some qualifications are necessary.

First, I am attempting to capture in print something that is in the process of creation. As such, there is necessarily the possibility, however unintended, of distortion. Second, in speaking of "ideology" as a unitary thing capable of being dissected, I do not mean to suggest that there is any coordinated effort at its creation. As with reform activities, the movement's emergent ideology is the product of diverse voices expressing similar but not identical points of view. Finally, the relationship between movement ideologues and structural reformers is not one of total harmony. As with many social movements (the women's movement, for example), the ideological creators of the happy death movement are considerably more "radical" and more "extreme" in their thinking than are the majority of movement participants and sympathizers.

The Evocation of Enemy

Enemies—real or created—are indigenous to social movements. As Turner and Killian have pointed out, a "movement is inconceivable apart from a vital sense that some established practice or mode of thought is *wrong* and ought to be replaced" (1972: 259). That sense of something wrong is sustained by a sense of "righteous indignation," a sense of injustice. "A sense of injustice that is vital enough to have consequences seems to require not only a situation that appears unfavorable by comparison with some reference group, but also an oppressor, so that the situation can be seen as a product of human will." In short, Turner and Killian argue (1972: 268), social movements need *enemies* (see also Gerlach and Hine, 1970: xvii).

Some movements—the nineteenth-century women's suffrage movement, for example—are "fortunate" in facing an opposition that is organized and articulate. The members of such organizations can be identified and personified. The oppressor is concrete; is real. But not all movements have "enemies" that are so clearly identifiable. It may be that the thing that is wrong, the practice that is abhorred is merely a de facto creation—simply the consequence of "the way things are done," with no one especially defending that way nor especially opposed to change but not especially anxious to undergo all the effort change entails, either. De facto enemies are not very useful in creating righteous indignation. They do not articulate any opposition. They do not seem in fact to be enemies at all. If they are to be useful to a movement, if they are to provide the emotional springboard for a sustained sense of injustice, they must be *evoked* by the movement itself. If they will not speak for themselves, they must be "articulated" by the movement.

There are undoubtedly many means for evoking an enemy, for articulating de facto opposition. The means utilized by the happy death movement is one of the simplest, and probably one of the most common. It involves doing only two things: set up an "ideal" and then point to the imperfect presumed real. Let us look at how this is done, first by critics of the modern family and then by happy death movement apologists.

The sociologist William Goode has described with insight the manner in which critics of contemporary family arrangements and practices evoke an ideal—what he calls the "classical family of Western nostalgia."

> It is a pretty picture of life down on grandma's farm. There are lots of happy children and many kinfolk live together in a large rambling house. Everyone works hard. Most of the food to be eaten during the winter is grown, preserved and stored on the farm. The family members repair their own equipment, and in general the household is economically self-sufficient. The family has many functions; it is the source of economic stability and religious, educational and vocational training. Father is stern and reserved and has the final decision in all important matters. Life is difficult, but harmonious because everyone knows his task and carries it out. All boys and girls marry, and marry young. Young people, especially the girls, are likely to be virginal at marriage and faithful afterward. Though the parents do not arrange their children's marriages, the elders do have the right to reject a suitor and have a strong hand in the final decision. After marriage, the couple lives harmoniously, either near the boy's parents or with them, for the couple is slated to inherit the farm. No one divorces. [Goode, 1970: 6]

Similarly, ideological creators of the happy death movement evoke "the classical death of Western (or other) nostalgia." There are many versions, but Elisabeth Kübler-Ross provides a classic example of the genre:

> I remember as a child [in Switzerland] the death of a farmer. He fell from a tree and was not expected to live. He asked simply to die at home, a wish that was granted without questioning. He called his daughters into the bedroom and spoke with each one of them alone for a few minutes. He arranged his affairs quietly, though he was in great pain, and distributed his belongings and his land, none of which was to be split until his wife should follow him in death. He also asked each of his children to share in the work, duties, and tasks that he had carried on until the time of the accident. He asked his friends to visit him once more, to bid good-bye to them. Although I was a small child at the time, he did not exclude me or my siblings. We were allowed to share in the preparations of the family just as we were permitted to grieve with them until he died. When he did die, he was left at home, in his own beloved home which he had built, and among his friends and neighbors who went to take a last look at him where he lay in the midst of flowers in the place he had lived in and loved so much. [Kübler-Ross, 1969: 5–6]

Having created an image of an ideal and allegedly "preferable" state of affairs, the ideological crafts-person then has only to describe the way in which the "presumed" real world fails to measure up. In so doing, the opposition is "articulated"; a social problem is *created* (Blumer, 1971).

For the happy death movement, the "presumed real" against which the ideal is measured involves a set of assertions about death and dying in contemporary America that I shall label, "the conventional view of death." It has been variously formulated, but essentially the view holds that America is a death-denying society, that death is a taboo topic, that death makes Americans uncomfortable so they run from it, that death is hidden

in America because Americans deny it, and so forth. The consequences of all this denial and repression are asserted to be quite
terrible: exorbitant funeral costs and barbaric funeral practices,
inhumane handling of dying in hospitals, ostracism of the dying
from the living, inauthentic communication with the fatally
ill, an unrealistic, mechanical, non-organic view of life, and so
forth. Philippe Ariès, widely cited in movement literature, provides an articulate example of the view:

> For thousands of years man was lord and master of his death, and the
> circumstances surrounding it. Today this has ceased to be so. ... Today
> nothing remains either of the sense that everyone has or should have
> of his impending death, or of the public solemnity surrounding the
> moment of death. What used to be appreciated is now hidden; what
> used to be solemn is now avoided. ... We have seen how modern
> society deprives man of his death, and how it allows him this privi-
> lege only if he does not use it to upset the living. In a reciprocal way,
> society forbids the living to appear moved by the death of others; it
> does not allow them either to weep for the deceased or to seem to
> miss them. [Ariès, 1974a: 136, 138, 143]

So does a recent (1977) advertising circular for a new "death
book": "The editors describe death as the contemporary taboo
that holds enormous terror for many persons." And a brochure
from the University of Minnesota's Center for Death Education
and Research:

> Every society *must* find the means to deal with this recurring crisis.
> "Death," as such, however, has been a "taboo" topic and hence has
> evoked little public discussion. People today are characteristically
> unwilling even to discuss the process of dying itself; they are even
> prone to avoid telling a dying person that he is, in fact, dying. This
> is partly a moral attitude: life is preferable to whatever may follow it,
> and one should not look forward to death unless he is in great pain.
>
> This moral attitude is shared by many professional people who
> work with or near the patients who die in our medical institutions.

> Most of the training that physicians and nurses receive in schools of medicine or nursing equips them principally for the technical aspects of dealing with patients. Little, if any instruction is offered on how to deal with the issue of death.

As many scholars have pointed out, the empirical evidence for all these assertions is something less than overwhelming. (See, for example, Dumont and Foss, 1972; Donaldson, 1972.) And one might consider it somewhat odd that the statement that death is a taboo topic in America should continue to be asserted in the face of nearly a decade of non-stop talking on the subject. But if one appreciates the *functions* these statements serve in enemy evocation, one can also appreciate that their questionable empirical basis is hardly a serious obstacle to endless repetition. The importance of the "conventional view of death"—of the conventional wisdom about death—as propounded over and over again by movement intellectuals, is not its "truth" but its utility.

Finally, it is important to appreciate the degree to which the happy death movement's "critique" of contemporary death attitudes and practices "meshes" with a broader intellectual tradition in the modern United States. I refer to the "humanistic-counterculture" denouncement of modern society in general, which denouncement emphasizes the Western world's dehumanizing, unemotional, technologically dominated, inauthentic, and constricted character. It may be that the movement's "conventional wisdom" draws much of its "believability" from what it shares with this broader tradition.[17]

The Components of a Craft of Dying

In a secular age, large numbers of humans confront the modern face of death unarmed with any certainties about what it might mean. A part of the ideological work of the happy death movement is, therefore, the construction of some larger meaning system into which the experiences modern humans are having with death may be placed. While the ideological edifice is at present incomplete, it is still possible, tentatively, to identify three components that may eventually be central to the finished structure. These are *immortality, positivity,* and *expressivity.*

Immortality

The fact of an afterlife has, in the late seventies, emerged as an increasingly central tenet of the happy death movement's ideology. What began in the early seventies as allusion has become assertion. What was born as vague suggestion is becoming creed. What could first be heard at conferences and workshops and symposia clothed in subtlety—as in the following:

> I said, "Russell, let go now; let go, easy, easy, this is it; let go and move on out now, please let go ... now!" And so he did. There was a sudden release of tension, the breathing stopped, his head dropped forward, and he was very still. The color paled, the expression left his face, and, after eight months, he had "broken free. ..." We all stayed up until dawn. *Soon after he died, the lightning flashed and by daylight it had begun to rain on the Mesa area of Santa Barbara, on a cliff overlooking the ocean on the south.* I sat by the window, deep in hazy thought, yet still and contemplative. *Was it really over?* What was "it", this awesome, marvelous thing we had been carried along by? *This was a cosmic experience,* I thought, and it doesn't matter if I ever do anything worthwhile again—ever. [Kerr, 1974: 29, emphasis added]

unfolds into stark forthrightness:

> Dr. Elisabeth Kübler-Ross who has counseled thousands of terminally ill patients, is convinced that "people don't really die."
>
> The 49 year old Swiss-born psychiatrist, author of *On Death and Dying* and two other books on death, says she knows "beyond the shadow of a doubt" there is life after death.

"This is not just the spooky stories of someone who has worked with too many dying patients, she said. "It is a good feeling to be able to say after many years that people don't really die." ["Specialist on Dying Says People Don't," *Sacramento Bee,* October 16, 1975][18]

Befitting a movement largely composed of presumably secular upper-middle-class professionals, the immortality claim rests not on revelation but on "research." That is, Kübler-Ross and others *know* there is an afterlife not as a consequence of any direct communication with a deity but because of "evidence," such as the following accounts, provided by the recovered "clinically dead."[19]

One patient, a 32-year-old female kidney dialysis patient, described her experience when she suffered liver and kidney failure, lapsed into a coma and had been given up for dead by doctors at Shands Teaching Hospital.

The woman found herself in a beautiful, serene environment where, across a border, she saw "people I knew who had died."

Without any fear or apprehension, the woman found herself approaching the border, she said, adding, "I would get almost across and they would seem to push me back. 'It's not time,' they said." [Life after Death Experiences Cited," *Sacramento Union,* August 2, 1977]

Barbara Feldman's experience is typical. "I was in the Intensive Care Unit following lung surgery. Suddenly I felt a sharp pain in my chest," she remembers. "I knew it was my heart. ... Then I heard one of the doctors say, 'We've lost her.'

"I noticed that a blue mist surrounded my body and was drifting up off the operating table. It was beautiful. I kept saying to myself: How can I be dead? I'm still conscious! ..."

"After a while I gave up trying to tell them I was alive. Then I realized that I was travelling through a long tunnel. There was a humming sound in my ears; not music, but it was pleasant. Up ahead was a brilliant light and I knew that I wanted to get to it. I had the most irresistible urge to become one with the light. I was travelling fast."

"Then an image of my three children appeared. I felt a tremendous tugging on my soul and I stopped travelling. I knew at that moment that I could either go on toward the light or return to my body. It was the hardest decision I ever had to make. I decided to return. ... I started descending toward my body and felt very sad. Then a voice, unlike anything I had ever heard, spoke. It said, 'You will be very happy for many years. And then you will return.'" [Panati, 1976: 78]

For some movement ideologues, then, the question of an afterlife is resolved; its exact character, however, remains undetermined. Despite the certainty of the three panelists at a late seventies seminar on "An Excursion into the Undiscovered Country,"[20] who undertook to chart "the different stages of consciousness experienced in the afterlife," most writers leave the issue open— perhaps reincarnation, perhaps a "spirit world," perhaps some ecstatic absorption into cosmic energy, perhaps something else altogether. On one aspect, however, there is consensus. Whatever the character of human immortality, it is *pleasant*. As such, the idea of immortality "fits" with a second component of movement ideology: positivity.

Positivity

One could argue that in its developing commitment to immortality as a component of its "craft of dying," the happy death movement is breaking away from the long trend of Western secularism and materialism.[21] Certainly, to the degree that the movement links with one or another version of mysticism, it would appear to move outside the stream of scientific rationalism that is the familiar milieu of most of its participants. In its commitment to the positive view, however—what I am calling "positivity"—the movement is firmly planted in the rich soil of tradition. If it is at all meaningful to speak of an "American culture"—or at least to speak of the culture of America's long-dominating Anglo group—then it is certainly plausible to argue that a recurring and important theme of that culture is positivity: a belief in progress, personal or societal; a belief in the possibility of solutions for all problems; a belief that life is potentially just and that one can get what one deserves.[22]

As a component of the ideology of the movement, positivity involves three interrelated assertions: (1) that the dying process may be the occasion for self-improvement and personality "growth" for the dying person; (2) that the dying process and subsequent grieving may be the occasion for self-improvement and personality "growth" for the family and friends of the dying/dead person; and (3) that death itself (the moment of death and what follows) may be blissful, serene, pleasurable, intensely contenting—perhaps even orgastic.

(1) An important message of movement rhetoric is that dying, for the dying, need not be dismal. If one is prepared to take advantage of the opportunities, dying and death may be—as Kübler-Ross subtitled her 1975 edited book—"the final stage of growth." For example, on the dust jacket of Stanley Keleman's widely and positively reviewed book, *Living Your Dying* (1974), we are asked: "Is there a person alive who isn't really curious about what dying is for them? Is there a person alive who wouldn't like to go to their dying full of excitement, without fear and without morbidity? This book tells you how." Similarly, in the introduction to her book, Marjorie McCoy promises to teach us how *To Die with Style:*

> My intention [in writing the book] has emerged from this new interest in death but at the same time I have sought a different, more radically positive way to view dying. I propose we look at death not primarily as a thing to be suffered but rather as an action to be anticipated and prepared for. Dying need not be equated with a watch

running down or a flower withering away, a stream drying up or a rock falling at last into a dark abyss. Why not, with Carl Jung, speak of "the *achievement* of death" and view dying as the final creative task of our lives? [1974: 16]

The quintessential version of this view is perhaps that of Mwalimu Imara:

We abhor and reject the moment when we will confront the nearness of our death. But the dying stage of our life can be experienced as *the most profound growth event of our total life's experience*. The shock, the pain and the anxiety are great, but if we are fortunate enough to have time to live and experience our own process, our arrival at a plateau of creative acceptance will be worth it. [1975: 149, emphasis added]

(2) One does not have to be dying oneself, however, to reap benefits. An ad for Peter Koestenbaum's *Is There an Answer to Death?* (1976) informs us that "a positive confrontation with death can be a personally liberating experience ... it can help us develop our individual identity and give us the security we need to live our lives courageously." That is, the dying and death of another is also an occasion for self-improvement and growth. Reflecting on the death of his son, Keith Kerr, a California marriage and family counsellor, writes:

In retrospect, even after some four years have elapsed, not all of the benefits, insights and awarenesses have become clear to us. It may seem strange to speak of "benefits" as coming from the death of anyone, not to mention a son or someone so close emotionally. The following have emerged to date: (1) A release from virtually all feelings of guilt. Whatever omissions in our rearing or relationship with Russell, they were compensated for and there are few regrets; (2) I, personally, began to shed—through our experience in his death—a lifelong compulsion to overwork and to "push" myself; (3) we felt we had "proven" ourselves in an act of fullest love and affection, and there was a consequent building of our self-esteem in a basic way; (4) personally, again, my own death became an absolute and eventual certainty to me through Russell's death. So not only did that reality emerge to me; I had looked death full in the face and it held no sense of foreboding or terror as I had in advance fantasized it would; (5) the tremendous energy depletion lasted for months. During that time, and up to the present, I was and am now totally unable to force my body or mind beyond their natural endurance limits. I withdraw and rest sooner, before being depleted of energy and I "listen" to my body more attentively. [Kerr, 1974: 29–30]

The same argument, more generally stated, is made by Roy Nichols and Jane Nichols in an article on funerals:

The ultimate goal of the grief work is to be able to remember without emotional pain and to be able to reinvest emotional surpluses. *While the experience of the grief work is difficult and slow and wearing, it is also enriching and fulfilling.* The most beautiful people we have known are those who have known defeat, known suffering, known struggle, known loss, and have found their way out of the depths. These persons have an appreciation, a sensitivity, and an understanding of life that fills them with compassion, gentleness, and a deep loving concern. Beautiful people do not just happen. [1975: 96, emphasis added]

(3) Finally, the positivity component offers the possibility that death itself and what ensues will be pleasurable. Again the experiences of the recovered "clinically dead" are brought forth as evidence (see above), but so are the perceptions of death witnesses.

Throughout human history, recorders of death-bed scenes tell of a frequent and strange phenomenon. They note that the visage of the newly deceased is quite often wreathed in a gentle smile or in a look of uncommon peace. Interpreters offer many explanations, all of them guesses. ... My guess is that the smile or look of peace reflects a satisfaction limited to men of any creed who died in peace. They expired without earthly strings of any kind choking their hearts and they realized that they had bequeathed no strings to choke the hearts of those they left behind. [Kavanaugh, 1972: 79]

In the above extract, Robert Kavanaugh, a former priest and current counselling psychologist offers only the hope for death as serene. Other writers have suggested a more tantalizing possibility. One example can stand for many:

> Death is the ultimate unification experience. As part of his eternal cycle and ceaseless becoming, man in death merges with himself, others, and all. ... There is an analogy here to the search for the perfect orgasm. Since time immemorial, or for as long as the recorded history of sexuality, man has attempted to perfect, prolong, and/or multiply the orgasm for himself and his partner. ... Death does not represent destruction, evil, meaningless oblivion, or the dark forces of man. It is the quintessence of what man has always desired most and what has been the chief motivational factor in his life, the search for, and repetition of, the spontaneous unification experiences he has encountered sporadically and at random during the course of his life and existence. It is the final, ultimate, and eternal experience of unity. [Gordon, 1970: 106, 108, 109]

As can be seen from these extracts, the positive character of dying and death is not simply given in the nature of things. Quite the contrary: the growth and self-improvement that may emerge out of the dying process—one's own or others—and the ecstasy of death itself are largely to be *achieved*. Understandably enough, writers vary in their prescriptions for salvation. But at least one element in those prescriptions is widely shared: one of the coins with which a "happy death" is purchased is *expressivity.*

Expressivity

The expressivity component of the happy death movement's emergent craft of dying specifies that whatever the emotions engendered by dying and death, they *should be ex pressed*. To suppress expression is to sacrifice the opportunities for "growth" that death provides.

Most people live their dying as they have lived their lives. People who rarely express themselves emotionally, or those whose lives are lived as misery and defeat, tend to die that way. People whose lives are rich in self-expression tend to die self-expressively. [Keleman, 1974: 4]

If survivors are made to feel ashamed of their spontaneous reactions to loss and the memory of the deceased, they suffer more distress than if they could acknowledge these in relation to others. In time, the failure to find opportunities for these grief efforts impairs the survivors' ability to cope with the recent as well as future bereavement. Every survivor needs opportunities to deal with his personal reactions to any death. The closer the relation, the greater the needs, and the greater the necessity of providing opportunities to talk about death, before, during, and long after termination. [Cutter, 1974: 128]

The emphasis on expressivity meshes nicely with the movement's utilization of "talk" (see above) as reform activity. It is important to stress, however, that expressivity calls not simply for talk but for *talk about one's varying emotional states, which talk "authentically" expresses those states*. Talk that is "mere" intellectualizing is proscribed. Expressivity demands, rather, a good deal of emotional temperature-taking and considerable concern for the genuineness of one's emotion. It is acceptable to feel very little, for example, only if this isn't "masking" some other denied feeling state. In sum, for the constructors of happy death movement ideology, the scenes of death and dying are more appropriately written by Eugene O'Neill than by Noël Coward. In the Afterword, I will consider, among other matters, some of the implications of that dramaturgic preference.

Afterword

In the preceding pages—pursuing some preliminary understandings about modern death activities—we have been led into two areas that are the domain of social scientists totally uninvolved in thanatological scholarship. In concluding this essay, then, I should like first to provide a more explicit link between this work and those areas: between my analysis of dying identity construction and the concerns of the *social psychology of roles* and between my description of happy death movement reform and ideology and the concerns of the *sociology of social movements*. I will, finally, consider some possible and *ironic consequences* of the success of individual and collective efforts to cope with the modern face of death and to fashion an appropriate craft of dying.

While there are certainly unique aspects to the construction of a *dying* role or identity, actors so engaged are involved in an enterprise that, in its broad outlines, is a common feature of modem life. The problem and potential of role construction is a recurrent challenge for contemporary humans not only because roles or identities generally have a heavy ad lib component to their enactment but, more importantly, because the modern world repeatedly generates new ways of being for which few if any models of enactment exist. If not since Mead, at least since the publication of Ralph Turner's 1962 essay on "Role Taking: Process Versus Conformity" (which critiqued the dominant static, ritualistic view of roles as set pieces embedded in "systems"), scholars, especially symbolic interactionists, have certainly been sensitive to the less than fully determined, creative, interactive and processual character of role behavior.[1] But they have not sufficiently appreciated, I think, the extent to which indeterminancy is built into role behavior as well, as a consequence of many roles having only recently emerged as part of the possibilities of the human condition. Being "dying," being a "liberated woman," being a "liberated man," being a "hippie businessman," being a "holistic medicine physician," being an "unemployed Ph.D."—as examples—are highly problematic activities.[2] Those who take on these new ways of being cannot simply adopt an extant model and then add their own ad lib flourishes. They must, rather, consciously select the elements or ingredients of their roles—shaping their *personae* from these ingredients and out of their struggle for control. Greater attention to this widespread activity by social scientists will tell us much, I believe, about the social psychology and structure of modem life.

I think it is accurate to say—without false humility—that while my description of the activities of the happy death movement makes a contribution to the sociology of death and dying, its value for the sociology of social movements is limited. I have not been able here to address myself to questions of movement origins nor to questions of organizational form or resources access and movement success, nor to questions of phases or stages of movement career, nor even to questions of recruitment and defection. But to say that a description is of limited value is not to say that it has no value at all. I have, I hope accurately, described some important aspects of a movement at a certain point in its history—a movement to which, as of this writing and to my knowledge, scholars of social movements have not attended. While the work here admittedly does not add to "social movement theory," it does, I judge, provide some of the necessary description out of which, combined with other descriptions of this and other movements, theory is generated and refined.

A last observation. It is difficult to judge how much of the activity we have been examining is mere "thanatological chic"— subject to waning interest as new foci of concern emerge[3]—and how much is firmly rooted in individual and organizational commitment. But as I suggested at the beginning of this essay, I think it is fair to say that in at least *some* of the construction of new actions and beliefs relative to death and dying, something of great consequence is occurring. In the face of death—that face that is peculiarly theirs—affluent Americans and other Westerners, individually and collectively, are creating a new craft of dying. As individuals struggle to fashion for themselves a dying identity, their successes and failures become part of the lore and legend that can be fashioned into reform and ideology. And as collective efforts at structural reform and at ideological creation develop, they become part of the milieu in which the construction of a dying identity occurs. Individually and collectively, modern humans seem to be "solving" the problems raised by the situation of modern death.

But solutions seem frequently—given the peculiarities of the human condition—to be double-edged swords. An accepted solution resolves a problem but it also reduces the availability of alternative solutions. When groups solve their problems, they seem also to bondage themselves to their own creations, to hedge themselves in with those creations. Thus, to the degree that the happy death movement achieves structural or ideological hegemony over the situation of modern death and dying, to the degree that it shapes that situation in its own image, to that degree it frees individual actors from one set of constraining contingencies only to surround them with another. If "natural death" philosophy comes to dominate medical practice, for example, the individual who wants to use every conceivable medical technology to prolong his or her life regardless of cost or efficacy becomes odd person out. If death talk is a constant feature of social interaction, persons who remain a little phobic on the topic face possible ridicule and isolation. If expressivity comes to be widely accepted as the only way to achieve a decent death, the emotionally reticent will find themselves under great pressure to "share."[4] If the idea that death and dying provide new opportunities for self-improvement becomes common currency, the chronic underachiever will find himself facing one more opportunity for failure.[5] Not "getting off' on death may become as déclassé as sexual unresponsiveness. Then, perhaps, a "dismal death" movement will arise to wipe the smile from the face of death and restore the "Grim Reaper" to his historic place of honor.

Epilogue

Ara A. Francis

I was a graduate student of Lyn Lofland at the University of California, Davis, in the 2000s, and by the time I came to study with her, her scholarship had moved away from death and dying. My interests were different too, rooted primarily in the sociology of families and emotion, so when we talked about *The Craft of Dying*, it was for other purposes. I remember conversations about role performances in the late-modern West, for example, and her use of the term "mixed type" to describe the happy death movement, but not much beyond that. It wasn't until 2017 that I re-read *The Craft of Dying* with an eye toward death studies. I was beginning a project on end-of-life doulas and death midwives, and the text blew me away. Lyn's analysis of death activism read as though it could have been written yesterday, and I wondered how that could be. In light of the happy death movement's ostensible achievements—the canonization of Elizabeth Kübler-Ross's work, for example, or the 1980s institutionalization and expansion of hospice—how is it that today's death-positive movement resembles so closely its progenitor of forty years ago and yet feels new to its participants? In the discussion that follows, I outline a few preliminary answers to that question, identifying factors that might help us to understand the movement's continued resonance and perennial challenges. I consider, too, what we as scholars and activists might take from *The Craft of Dying* going forward.

Like its 1970s counterpart, today's death-positive movement is diffuse and uncoordinated, comprised of individuals and organizations working in different arenas with separate but overlapping aims. At death cafes designed to raise awareness about mortality, strangers gather to chat about death over tea and cake. Weekend-long death salons offer death-themed talks, performances and foods. Courses in end-of-life doula care and death midwifery are populated by women interested in facing their own mortality, preparing to care for aging loved ones, or hoping to start their own alternative death care businesses. Entrepreneurs in the death trade now offer home funerals, green burials and a growing number of disposition alternatives. Consumers can buy apps for their phones that record their end-of-life preferences or remind them at regular intervals that they're going to die. And the death with dignity movement marches on, in the last five years adding California, Colorado, Hawaii, Vermont, and Washington, D.C., to the list of U.S. jurisdictions with medical aid in dying statutes.

Participants in the contemporary death-positive movement adhere to two of the basic tenets that Lofland identified: if we are to die better, its participants suggest, we must talk about it and legislate it. These efforts look much as they did forty years ago, with the caveat that they now have greater precedent and, thus, a longer tradition to draw from. For example, death-with-dignity advocates now can wield data from jurisdictions where physician-assisted suicide is legal, arguing that "Medical aid in dying has been safely practiced in six states for a combined 40 years ... [and not a] single case of abuse or coercion nor any criminal or disciplinary charges have been filed" (Compassion and Choices, 2017). Similarly, expressivity is assumed to be a necessary feature of the good death and healthy grief. For example, three of the eight tenets that define "The Order of the Good Death"—a group that showcases contemporary death activism—are premised explicitly on communication:

2. I believe that the culture of silence around death should be broken through discussion, gatherings, art, innovation, and scholarship.

3. I believe that talking about and engaging with my inevitable death is not morbid, but displays a natural curiosity about the human condition. [...]

7. I believe that my family and friends should know my end-of-life wishes, and that I should have the necessary paperwork to back-up those wishes. [Order of the Good Death, 2018]

Scholarly and psychotherapeutic understandings of grief have moved away from the stage-based model, healthy/pathological binary, and notions of "closure" that Lyn describes (Rothaupt and Becker, 2007). Nonetheless, talking about death is still assumed to be a fundamentally good thing. Robert A. Neimeyer, a widely known scholar of grief therapy, spoke about death salons in a piece for *The Atlantic*: "Whether frank and courageous conversation about death and loss takes place in a classroom, therapist's office, church or temple, or the local Starbucks ... my guess is that it can help us explore and articulate frameworks of meaning for negotiating the often unwelcome transitions that confront us all" (Hayasaki, 2013).

The third tenet that Lofland identifies—the rearrangement of death and dying—manifests differently today than it did when *The Craft of Dying* was published, in part because of the availability of hospice. As Lofland notes, efforts in the United States to relocate death to private homes or freestanding hospices were, at the time she was writing, "only minimally successful." More challenging to pioneers than the lukewarm reception of medical professionals, though, were the financial logistics of hospice operation. In the 1970s most hospices were small, grassroots organizations that relied heavily on volunteers. Their limited budgets were comprised of grants and donations, which made for a tenuous existence (Abel, 1986; Livne, 2014). By the end of that decade, advocates began framing hospice as a cost-effective alternative to mainstream care, and in 1982, Congress approved the Tax Equity and Fiscal Responsibility Act (TEFRA), granting Medicare coverage for hospice. This catalyzed the expansion of hospice, which now attends to approximately one-third of all deaths in the United States (National Hospice and Palliative Care Organization, 2018).

Rather than advocating for the spatial reorganization of death, then, today's death-positive activists argue for the continued diversification of end-of-life options and seek to educate people about their choices. This orientation to end-of-life care is evident in the emerging roles of end-of-life doulas and death midwives, whose work it is to co-construct and help carry out each client's particular vision of a good death or disposition. At the same time that they emphasize choice, courses in alternative death care also tend to promote an idealized, "natural death"—a death that takes place at home with the assistance of hospice and minimal interference from medical or funeral professionals. In this way, the aims of alternative death care today are strikingly similar to those of early hospice organizers such as Cicely Saunders, Elisabeth Kübler-Ross, and Florence Wald. Like their 1970s counterparts, contemporary advocates are critical of death's medicalization, possess an anti-institutional sentiment, champion personalized care, and see dying as an opportunity for psychosocial growth and affirmation.

Some death-positive educators and activists recognize their indebtedness to the 1970s death movement, as well the AIDS-focused activism in the era that followed. Nonetheless, many participants experience death positivity as new, a misconception that news accounts continually reinforce. "Death Is Having a Moment," a 2013 piece in *The Atlantic* heralded, describing the movement as "recent," "growing" and "spreading" (Hayasaki, 2013). "Once the province of goth subculture, death is having a moment in the sun," the *New York Times* announced in the byline of a 2018 article titled "The Positive Death Movement Comes to Life" (Leland, 2018). The premium of newness in popular media notwithstanding, how did this movement come to feel new when the essential tenor of death-positive activism has not changed in more than forty years?

It is tempting to argue that the death-positive movement resonates just as much now as it did in the 1970s because death denial in the global North has proved intractable. However, just as John Troyer points out in his introduction, assertions regarding a death taboo are empirically dubious, just as they were when *The Craft of Dying* was first published. Death's frequent presence in both private and public discourse suggests that the denial thesis is, at best, overstated and under-nuanced (Walter, 1991). The degree to which people in the postmodern West are comfortable acknowledging and talking about death appears to be widely variable and rooted in social contexts such as race, class, gender and occupation. Indeed, it is likely that the death taboo thesis remains popular because of—not in spite of—the happy death movement, which led to the canonization of works such as Elisabeth Kübler-Ross's *On Death and Dying* (1969) and Ernest Becker's *Denial of Death* (1973), both of which propagated the death-denial thesis.

There are at least two factors that might help to explain the death-positive movement's current salience, the first of which is demographic. Lofland argues that one potential reason for the surge of death discourse in the 1970s was that the proportion of people confronting the new face of death had reached a certain threshold that gave way to public expression. In other words, changes in the conditions of death and dying had been underway for decades, but it took a while for those changes to manifest in enough people's experiences to culminate in public conversation. A similar argument could be made today about the growing proportion of baby boomers who have experienced a serious health crisis or witnessed the death of a parent or partner. Happy death discourse has been a part of our Western cultural repertoire for the past 40 years, but it is increasingly relevant to the large generation of people born between 1946 and 1964. Indeed, the countercultural, choice-driven narrative that characterizes death positivity might have special appeal for baby boomers who came of age in the 1970s.

A second factor is the current state of hospice care. The alternative death care dimension of today's death-positive movement has emerged, in part, as a response to the failure of hospice to make good on its promise of holistic, person-centered care. Some of the people who offer courses in death midwifery and end-of-life doula care started their careers as hospice social workers or nurses but left when institutional constraints prevented them from delivering the care they had envisioned. Although the Medicare benefit afforded hospice organizations greater stability and allowed them to serve a larger swath of the American population, it also transformed the very nature of hospice care. TEFRA hastened the institutionalization of hospice and undermined the potentially revolutionary dimensions of its vision (Abel, 1986). As hospices entered into partnerships with hospitals, home health agencies, and nursing homes, they bent to the regulations and procedures of those parent organizations. TEFRA itself redefined hospice's scope, stipulating that only patients with six months or less to live may receive coverage and that hospices may not offer curative or life-sustaining treatment. Because Medicare issues a lump-sum payment for each day a patient is served, regardless of what services are actually rendered, hospices absorb the loss when the cost of a day's treatment exceeds that lump-sum and receive a surplus when the cost remains below it. Some hospices have sought to increase their surplus by deploying an economies-of-scale approach, taking on more patients without increasing their staff or resources (Livne, 2014). Consequently, hospice care is now managed care and, in many cases, resembles other parts of the mainstream U.S. health care system. Evidence suggests that the quality and frequency of hospice care is uneven and that, particularly when patients are admitted to hospice too late, their needs go unmet (Schockett et al., 2005; Teno et al., 2016; Makaroun et al., 2018). In contrast with the round-the-clock care envisioned by hospice pioneers (Abel 1986), some hospice patients do not receive assistance even in the two days prior to death when their needs are usually highest (Teno et al., 2016). For reasons still debated in the literature, these shortcomings are disproportionately borne by patients of color and patients who are poor (Teno et al., 2016).

The trajectory of hospice from a grassroots, anti-industrial movement to a part of the mainstream health care marketplace highlights a key shortcoming of the happy death movement: movement leaders focused on changing people's ideas about dying and assumed that institutional change would follow. As the history of hospice in the United States so clearly illustrates, institutional logics are obstinate and can persist even in the absence of ideological support. In the end, it was not enough for hospice personnel to present hospital and nursing home staff with an alternative model for end-of-life care. Without proper institutional arrangements in the form of economic and regulatory support, hospices were as just likely to take on the characteristics of hospitals and nursing homes as they were to revolutionize those systems, regardless of patients' or care providers' wishes.

Nonetheless, hospice faced challenges beyond its institutionalization and integration into the mainstream health care system. Although hospice has, since its inception, provided a meaningful alternative to the protracted suffering we have come to associate with death in Intensive Care Units, its ideals have always been difficult to attain. As illustrated in Emily Abel's (2018) analysis of the records kept by hospice founder Florence Wald, many early patients and their families rejected expressivity and, despite Wald's best efforts, remained embroiled in intractable conflicts. Although the hospice model was premised on knowing when a person would no longer benefit from curative treatment, making that determination sometimes proved impossible. Many of Wald's patients lacked family support or had loved ones who felt overwhelmed by the prospect of caring for them, and some patients died terrible deaths, even with the full support of Wald and her colleagues. In short, pioneers like Wald held tightly to their vision of a good death, even when their own experiences highlighted the limitations of that vision vis-à-vis the lived experiences of dying people. That their ideals grew out of their own biographies as white, middle-class women also went unnoticed.

There is no doubt that today's death-positive movement responds to a pressing social concern: there is widespread recognition, well-supported by empirical data, that the U.S. health care system does not meet people's needs at the end of life (Institute of Medicine, Committee on Approaching Death 2015). At the same time, it is not at all clear that talking about, planning for, or hiring people to help us coordinate our dying will address the systemic problems that lead to bad dying in the first place. Thus, Lofland's critique of the happy death movement has much to teach us about the blind spots of contemporary death activism. As she points out, death positivity is premised on an ethos that is not shared by all people. Self-reflection and self-expression, choice and personal customization, and the desire for what is ostensibly "natural" are culturally and historically specific values that resonate especially strongly with affluent whites. As Katharine McCabe (2016) argues in her study of birth midwives and doulas, these forms of empowerment do not pose significant challenges to the health care system insofar as they promote self-sufficiency and personal responsibility, allow for divestment in public resources and mask systemic inequalities that contextualize and constrain the choice-making of non-privileged consumers. If empowerment hinges on purchasing the services of independent practitioners, then empowerment itself is act of consumption, and this model offers no purchase for questioning why our medical system fails people so routinely. What's more, the narrow ideals of "natural dying" frame as problematic some people's genuine desire for intensive medical intervention.

Much like the founders of hospice, today's end-of-life doulas and death midwives face pressures that threaten to undermine the more radical tenets of their work. What is special about these practitioners is that they are not meant to bring a professional agenda to the bedsides of dying people. Instead, doulas and midwives are defined by their authenticity, heart, humanness and a willingness to prioritize above all else the dying person's needs and desires, whatever those might be. Some of these practitioners aim to "teach themselves out of a job," as they work to return end-of-life caregiving to the hands of loved ones and community members. At the same time, alternative death care educators are seeking occupational legitimacy for death midwives and end-of-life doulas, and they are doing so by engaging in the tried-and-true methods of professionalization: by seeking to convince people that end-of-life doulas and death midwives offer a valuable commodity, by codifying a scope of practice, and by standardizing training and certification. These two dimensions of alternative death care—the commitment to humanizing care, on the one hand, and the pressure to professionalize, on the other—are in tension with one another. As one pioneer put it to me during an interview, "How are you going to teach heart?" Can the commodification of this work be reconciled with the countercultural aim of reskilling loved ones in end-of-life care? And if end-of-life doulas partner with hospice organizations, as some have started to do, how will they navigate systems that are organized to minimize costs?

Whatever the future of alternative end-of-life care, *The Craft of Dying* offers at least two important lessons to contemporary death activists and scholars. The first is an unflinching look at how contemporary visions of good dying are the products of particular people, places, and times. Death-positive rhetoric continues to position "natural dying" as a universally shared human experience, one that is rooted in our premodern past. Doing so obscures how the movement's objectives and challenges are distinctly postmodern. In the same vein, the movement must consider how its tenets reflect the lived experiences of its leaders, most of whom are middle-class, college-educated white women. Eager to bring conversations about dying to marginalized communities, for example, leaders sometimes fail to recognize conversations already taking place. How might the death-positive movement engage with the death activism of Black Lives Matter? Lofland's second offering is a stubborn refusal to be easily seduced by the promise of happy dying. This is not to say that people cannot find happiness, peace, intimacy, beauty or closure in death or that we should not try to help people die well. Rather, it is to recognize that our ability to orchestrate those experiences is limited by a host of factors beyond our control. Perhaps more importantly, history suggests that change must take place at the level of institutions, not just individuals. How might the death-positive movement engage more holistically with policy decisions pertaining to our health care system? In any case, the clear-eyed, critical perspective that Lofland models in *The Craft of Dying* provides a good point of departure for any undertaking meant to change the way people die.

References

Abel, Emily K. (1986) "The hospice movement: institutionalizing innovation." *International Journal of Health Services: Planning, Administration, Evaluation* 16, 1: 71–85.

—— (2018) *Prelude to Hospice: Florence Wald, Dying People and Their Families*. Rutgers University Press.

Becker, Ernest (1973) *The Denial of Death*. The Free Press.

Compassion and Choices (2017) "The facts about medical aid in dying." Retrieved August 31, 2018 (https://www.compassionandchoices.org/wp-content/uploads/2016/02/One-Pager-The-Facts-About-Medical-Aid-in-Dying-FINAL-8.29.17-Approved-for-Public-Distribution.pdf).

Hayasaki, Erika (2013) "Death is having a moment." *The Atlantic*. Retrieved August 31, 2018 (https://www.theatlantic.com/health/archive/2013/10/death-is-having-a-moment/280777).

Institute of Medicine, Committee on Approaching Death (2015) "Dying in America: improving quality and honoring individual preferences near the end of life." The National Academies Press.

Kübler-Ross, Elisabeth (1969) *On Death and Dying: What the Dying Have to Teach Doctors, Nurses, Clergy, and Their Own Families*. Macmillan.

Leland, John (2018) "The positive death movement comes to life." *New York Times*. Retrieved August 31, 2018 (https://www.nytimes.com/2018/06/22/nyregion/the-positive-death-movement-comes-to-life.html).

Livne, Roi (2014) "Economies of dying: the moralization of economic scarcity in U.S. hospice care." *American Sociological Review* 79, 5: 888–911.

Makaroun, Lena K., Joan M. Teno, Vicki A. Freedman, Judith D. Kasper, Pedro Gozalo and Vincent Mor (2018) "Late transitions and bereaved family member perceptions of quality of end-of-life care." *Journal of the American Geriatrics*.

McCabe, Katharine (2016) "Mothercraft: birth work and the making of neoliberal mothers." *Social Science & Medicine* 162: 177–184.

National Hospice and Palliative Care Organization (2018) "NHPCO facts and figures: hospice care in America." Alexandria, VA.

Order of the Good Death (2018) "Death positive." Retrieved August 31, 2018. (http://www.orderofthegooddeath.com/death-positive).

Rothaupt, Jeanne W., and Kent Becker (2007) "A literature review of Western bereavement theory: from decathecting to continuing bonds." *Family Journal* 15, 1: 6–15.

Schockett, Erica R., Joan M. Teno, Susan C. Miller and Brad Stuart (2005) "Late referral to hospice and bereaved family member perception of quality of end-of-life care." *Journal of Pain and Symptom Management* 30, 5: 400–407.

Teno, Joan M., Mike Plotzke, Thomas Christian and Pedro Gozalo (2016) "Examining variation in hospice visits by professional staff in the last 2 days of life." *JAMA Internal Medicine* 176, 3: 364–370.

Walter, Tony (1991) "Modern death: taboo or not taboo?" *Sociology* 25, 2: 293–310.

Notes

Preface

1. "Paper Back Talk," *New York Times Book Review* (August 29, 1976): 23.

2. "High Society Rag," *Newsweek* (September 8, 1975): 48, emphasis added.

3. Charmaz (in press) and Wood (1976a) both address this question. See also Crane (1975): 8–10; Kastenbaum (1977).

Part I

1. The possibility that death may not be "inevitable" in the future (see note 2) does not, of course, gainsay the accuracy of this statement relative both to the past and to the current situation.

2. The question of whether death—at least death as a consequence of the aging process and its associated degenerative diseases—can in fact be eliminated is taken very seriously by some researchers. See, for example, "Can Aging Be Cured?" *Newsweek* (April 16, 1973): 54–55, 57–58, 63–64, 66. See also, "San Diego Group Opens Campaign to Postpone or Even Conquer Death" *Davis Enterprise* (November 25, 1976). The elimination of death is also, of course, an article of faith among believers in Cryonics who advocate freezing the "clinically dead" until medical science progresses to the point where reanimation is both possible and advisable.

For a thorough study of the Cryonics' belief system and organization, see Sheskin (in press).

3. It is because, I would suggest, groups get used to the particular death profile that is characteristic for them that they develop conceptions of meaning—*less* or *senseless* deaths. That is, deaths that are outside the profile, that differ from the usual, may not be contained or explained very well by the group's practices or beliefs. They remain problematic to the group. Thus the death of a baby among a people for whom baby deaths are a usual occurrence, for example, is an event conceived quite differently from the way it is among a people whose babies almost all survive ... (Ariès, 1962). Affluent Americans appear to find death among the old "understandable" (although aspects of the dying may be problematic) but are less at ease with the deaths of young adults, the latter frequently evoking such epitaphs as "meaningless" or "senseless." Blauner (1966) provides an insightful discussion of this and related topics. See also Weisman (1973).

4. On the link between dissatisfactions and social movements, see Blumer (1969b). I do not mean to imply a rigid demographic deter- minism here. A group's actions and beliefs relative to death—its craft of dying—are certainly related to such matters as life expectancy, death causation, death rates by age group, death tempo and so forth. But that relationship is neither simple nor unidirectional, for death demograph- ics are themselves created by a group's actions and beliefs not only rela- tive to death but relative to life. As Berger and Luckmann note,

> A pointed illustration of society's limitation of the organism's biological pos- sibilities is longevity. Life expectancy varies with social location. Even in con- temporary American society there is considerable discrepancy between the life expectancies of lower-class and upper-class individuals. furthermore, both the incidence and the character of pathology vary with social location. Lower-class individuals are ill more frequently than upper-class individuals, in addition, they have different illnesses. In other words, society determines how long and in what manner the individual organism shall live. [1967: 181]

Stannard (1973: 5) hints further at the complexity of the relationship between mortality and society when he notes that devout New England Puritans were importantly preoccupied by death, much as were the men and women of the late Middle Ages in Europe. But unlike these medieval populations, the Puritan was not exposed to an "inordinate amount of death." In fact, even as compared with his relatives in England, he lived a healthier and longer life. See also Gove (1973); Kastenbaum and Aisenberg (1972): chs. 10–15; Parkes (1964); Vernon (1970); Vernon and Waddell (1974).

Links between a group's particular experience of death and its culture and organization of death have previously been explored by many scholars for many groups and times, although, perhaps because of the overwhelming character of its death experience and death preoccupation, medieval Europe, especially late fourteenth-century Europe, has received a major share of the attention. Among the many works exploring the linkage in this and other periods, see Ariès, (1974b); Douce (1833), Hertz (1960); Huizinga (1963); Kastenbaum and Aisenberg, (1972).

5. This activity is not limited to the United States although I shall limit my analysis primarily to events occurring within its boundaries. Especially relative to new organizational forms, such as the hospice (see pp. 84–85) much activity has emanated from England. And a recent spurt of publications from the Continent suggests that increasing attention to matters of death and dying is a European phenomenon (Lottman, 1975). It would be surprising if it were otherwise. As numerous scholars have noted, the conditions that produce these activities are, to a considerable degree, present throughout the advanced industrialized world.

6. I shall discuss this further in part II.

7. My definition differs considerably from Sudnow's (1967: 63–65) more precise formulation, in the main because his definition is linked to the particular organizational setting that created it (hospital) while mine attempts to transcend any particular institutional sphere and capture the broader "popular understanding." See also Glaser and Strauss (1968): ch. 3; Kalish (1970).

8. In especially highlighting the prolonged-dying aspect of changing mortality patterns, I am shifting emphasis away from the more usual focus on increased longevity. While I do not wish to underplay the importance of this latter shift, and it is certainly—along with prolonged

dying—part of a complex of patterns that mark off the modern experience of death from the premodern experience, for my purposes, the fact that more people are dying longer is more interesting than the fact that more of them are living longer. For very fine analyses of the "mortality revolution" that conceive the premodern experience in terms rather different from mine but on which I have relied extensively, see Goldscheider (1971, 1976); and Blauner (1966). See also Ariès (1974b); Kastenbaum and Aisenberg (1972): ch. 8; and Wrigley (1969).

Of course, in capturing enormously complex mortality patterns in simple "premodern/modern" contrast terms as I and many other scholars do, much variation within each pattern is lost. Without underplaying the importance of this variation, I would nonetheless argue that *for present purposes* (and for the purposes of other scholars who have done the same) such oversimplication and thus distortion is both justified and fruitful.

9. This list is not necessarily exhaustive nor are the items necessarily exclusive. And the set of conditions may not be the most felicitous one could devise. I have, however, found this listing useful. One does not, by the way, need to reify Western medical categories or theories to recognize that as a way of constructing reality and relative to certain specifiable outcomes, Western medicine has been remarkably efficacious.

10. This terminology is borrowed from Glaser and Strauss (1968), although my interest in "trajectories" remains far more limited than theirs, concerned as it is primarily with the property of duration. They extended their interest to include "shape."

11. Smallpox, for example, is reported to have destroyed 25 to 30% of medieval Europe's population in a single epidemic and to have taken one-third of Iceland's population in 1707, and three-and-a-half million Mexicans following the introduction of the disease in 1520. I am being somewhat loose with the language in equating "communicable" or "infectious" with "acute." Some acute illnesses, viral pneumonia, for example, are not infectious. And some infectious conditions—athlete's foot comes to mind—might better be conceived as chronic. But the overlap is sufficient, I think, to keep distortions to a minimum.

12. For example, Lerner reports that in 1900, major communicable diseases were leading causes of death in the United States (1970: 12–13). One might point also to such anecdotal evidence as Dorothy George's comments about the decline in London in the 1700s of mortality from such previously important killers as dysentery and intermittent fever (1965: 27). The high infant mortality rates in the premodern world and the considerable incidence of deaths in childbirth lend further support to the argument.

13. See, for example, Bowra et al. (1952); Byrne (1961); Carcopino (1940); Holmes (1966); Lacroix (1963); Lenski (1970); Mayhew (1950); Miller (1966); Rowling (1968); Silver (1967); and Sjoberg (1960). On executions specifically, see Laurence (1960); and J. Lofland (1976b, 1977).

14. See pp. 88–92 on the uses of this evocation. The issues of whether death is "accepted or denied" by contemporary Americans, whether other groups in other places and other times have been "more accepting," whether acceptance or denial is a good thing or a bad thing, what constitutes acceptance or denial anyway, and related matters have been subject to considerable and heated debate in the "death literature." For a review of some aspects of the controversy, see Dumont and Foss (1972). See also, Donaldson (1972). Marcuse (1959) is one of the few writers to discuss the "sinister" aspects of an attitude of "death acceptance." Marshall (1975a) makes a major step in a more sophisticated formulation of the issues.

15. See, for example, Ariès (1974b); Benedict (1934); Hicks (1975); Levy (1973); Malinowski (1954); and Simmons (1945).

16. While I am primarily discussing the United States' experience, the mortality patterns to which I refer are generally typical of all advanced industrialized countries. Lerner, reporting on Hillery et al. (1968) notes that "in the demographically transitional countries (low death rates but high birth rates) the degenerative diseases account for less than one-third of all deaths, whereas in the demographically mature countries (both death rates and birth rates low [advanced industrialized nations mostly]) these diseases account for just under two-thirds of the total" (1970: 16). See further, Preston et al. (1972).

17. Smallpox may, in fact, shortly be totally eradicated worldwide. See Honig (1975). See also "Conquest of Smallpox Worldwide Is Imminent" *Sacramento Bee* (September 12, 1976).

18. See also, the materials in Dingle (1973: 82).

19. See, for example, "Heart Disease Death Rate Drops," *San Francisco Chronicle* (May 6, 1974); "Three Extra Years for Kids Born Today," *Sacramento Union* (July 26, 1977).

20. Questions of whether such sophistication is good or even efficient are not at issue here and will be left aside.

21. But good general discussions can be found in Hendin (1973); and Langone (1974).

22. The relevant literature is already enormous and growing steadily. Valuable discussions are to be found in Behnke and Bok, eds. (1975); Downing, ed. (1969); Kohl (1974); Maguire (1974); Mannes (1973); Russell (1975).

23. This is the message of much of the American Cancer Society's advertising.

24. Ironically, some few may now be dead who in times past would merely be dying. Mant (1976), in discussing the historic fear and problem of premature burial, notes that

> Some of these [trance-like] states lasted for several days, and the absence of any sign of putrefaction resulted in continued resuscitative measures. [These measures], for instance, keeping the body warm and applying mustard poultices, would, if the person had been dead, have accelerated the onset of putrefaction. These trance-like states, like the fashionable "vapors" of the nineteenth century, appear to have disappeared in the twentieth century. However, should a person in such a trance-like state be certified dead today, his chances of resurrection would be diminished because bodies are not usually kept at home but transferred to refrigerators in public mortuaries or undertakers' chapels, where any trance-like state would rapidly become permanent! [1976: 223]

See Veatch (1976a and b); Hendin (1973); Capron and Kass (1972–73); and Winter, ed. (1969) for a good introduction to the medical, ethical and legal difficulties engendered by current technology, conceptions, and practices.

25. On this topic, see Crane (1975); Coombs and Powers (1976); Parsons et al. (1973); Parsons and Lidz (1967); and Howard and Scott (1965–66).

26. A point that many commentators on the contemporary death scene seem unable or unwilling to grasp. The writings of many hint that dying is bureaucratized as a consequence of some conspiracy of cruelty or avoidance.

27. On American secularity relative to death, see Spiegel (1964). More generally, see Glock and Stark (1965); and Wilson (1966), especially part I, "The Pattern of Secularization." On the premodern/modern alteration in the status of the "sacred," see Childe (1942); Lenski (1970); Sjoberg (1960).

28. This is not to say that premodern groups did not provide instructions in "how to act" during the relatively brief duration of dying. Many did, in detailed form (see part II, pp. 48–49).

29. It should be noted that modern societies are not the first groups to segregate their dying into specialized institutions. The institution of the "dying house" or "death house" has been a fairly widespread phenomenon. Such houses were not, however, bureaucratically organized, nor were they intended to serve any interventionist or activist goals, but were simply a special setting in which fatalism toward the dying could be expressed.

30. Existentialism might be viewed as a culturally available set of beliefs that places dying and death within an "explanatory" context. I suspect, however, that its emphasis on transcending despair through accepting meaninglessness is rather too grim for it to be amenable as a day-to-day "living with" philosophy to more than a handful.

31. See part III, pp. 88–92 regarding the functions of such evocations.

32. This account ignores—as do the assertions of most critics of American death practices—the necessarily heightened death awareness and salience created by 20th century wars. The complex question of the interrelationship between levels and areas of "death talk" and war remains unexplored.

Part II

1. I am borrowing here from J. Lofland (1976a): ch. 9, 139–140, although I use the term somewhat differently than he. By role enterprise, Lofland refers to the creation of the role, per se, a category of being. I am referring to the creation of the particular components of that category. I trust the two usages of the term are not incompatible.

2. I shall use "role" and "identity" interchangeably to refer simply to a category of being. I am cognizant of the many complex and finely crafted definitions and specifications of these terms. For my purposes, however, they are not useful. Wood (1972) is an early and useful review of much of the relevant literature on "being dying."

3. See Glaser and Strauss (1965a, 1971).

4. At least this is true in modern societies that tend to have no social intercourse with their dead. Whether the dead are helpful or not in groups who maintain contact, I cannot say.

5. The usual absence of veterans of a transitional role that more and more humans must face may account for some of the growing interest in the experiences of the "clinical dead" who then revive and of those who "almost die." See, for example, Moody (1975); Hunter (1967); Noyes and Kletti (1972); Panati (1976); and Snell (1967).

6. The entrenchment of the gate-keepers as certifiers of the dying identity may help to account for some of the difficulty Western medicine has in understanding so-called prescient death, that is, death from no obvious physical cause but that is predicted beforehand by the person who dies. See, for example, Barber (1961); Cannon (1942); Walter (1944); Weisman and Hackett (1976); Yawger (1936); Richter (1959).

7. Moore and Tumin's "Some Social Functions of Ignorance" (1949) can fruitfully be read for clues to the "utility" of the closed awareness context. Kalish (1970) is an insightful discussion of some of the complexities of "learning of dying."

8. As an example, a eulogy in *The New Yorker* reports that "even after months had passed, and years, he refused to subside into invalidism but instead chose to believe that he was merely taking time out from his real life, and from his writing. ... Yet up to the time he died, he [though of himself as] a young man who one day might wake up, his health restored, walk down the street again, look around him, return home, and embark on some new—and flawless—comic enterprise" (Anonymous, 1975).

9. See, for example, Schulz and Aderman (1974); Pattison (1967); Williams (1973); Gustafson (1972); Rothenberg (1961). Wood (1976b) and Charmaz (1976a) provide fully *sociological* critiques of Kübler-Ross. Charmaz (1977) provides considerable insight into the interrelationship between time and identity.

10. As true of the category "dead" as of "dying" perhaps. Aubert and White (1968) have suggested that sleep may be viewed as a "rehearsal for death."

11. This is but one of the many "dying script" examples to be found in Ariès (1974b). On Puritan prescriptions, see Stannard (1973). See also Simmons (1945). The *Ars Moriendi* or "book of the craft of dying" was a many versioned set of detailed instructions to medieval Christians on dying well. On the *Ars Moriendi,* see Camper, ed. (1917); and O'Connor (1942). Barbellion (1919 and 1920) are among the few accounts of prolonged dying in an essentially premodern death situation.

12. This freedom is certainly not total. It is profoundly infringed upon by others and by circumstances as I will discuss below. On the ad lib possibilities in role enactment, see Secord and Backman (1974): 413–418.

13. As will become obvious, these dimensions are importantly interrelated. For analytic purposes, however, their separation is useful. For a quite different analysis of the "tasks of the dying person," see Kalish (1970).

14. One can see here a pattern of change through time in space devoted to dying: minimal devotion when the role is first entered, increasing

attention as the actor gets closer and closer to death. Undoubtedly, this pattern is one of the more frequent.

15. Fox (1959) is a study of a special hospital ward composed entirely of "dying" persons. Oddly enough, the book reports little in the way of talk about the participants' shared passage.

16. See, for example, Marshall (1975b, 1976); Gubrium (1975, 1976); Glaser and Strauss (1965b, 1968); Strauss and Glaser (1970).

17. On Chuck McCracken, see "Why I decided to die with dignity," *The National Enquirer* (October 28, 1975). On Lois Jaffe, see MacLeod (1975). On Della Kilkenny, see Demuth (1973). On Sharon Baptista, see "Under the Shadow of Death," *The Sacramento Bee* (January 22, 1975). On Nancy Robinson, see Durant (1976). On Delmar Stuermer, see "A Sick Man's Plea to End His Misery and His Life," *San Francisco Sunday Examiner and Chronicle* (October 19, 1975). On Ruth Howard, see Cohn (1975).

18. See J. Lofland (1976b and 1977) on the expression of "stance" by condemned in historic executions. Examples of extant choices are found most easily, unsurprisingly enough, among media deaths. With the exception of Strauss and Glaser's *Anguish* (1970), where the stance (if any) of the central character, Mrs. Abel, might be described as "whining" (discussed below), sociological studies of dying in hospitals tend not to convey this dimension of the role. This may simply be a consequence of disattention. Or, it may occur because bureaucratic settings themselves tend to suppress the expression of any stance beyond the cooperative compliance they wish to evoke. (See, for example, Glaser and Strauss, 1965b.)

19. Glaser and Strauss (1968) have analyzed the role expectations of hospital personnel relative to the dying and have looked at some of the techniques used to extract compliance with these expectations. While it remains true, as indicated above, that no precise cultural script exists for the contemporary dying role, it is expected that among groups for whom the dying role is continually relevant, some form of "script" or set of expectations will emerge. In addition to Glaser and Strauss, see Marshall (1976) on nursing homes and Hochschild (1973) and Marshall (1975b, 1976) on retirement communities.

20. See, for example, Marshall (1975b, 1976).

21. As the burgeoning literature on "death with dignity," "euthanasia," the "rights" of the dying and similar topics makes testimony. See, for example, Downing, ed. (1969); Maguire (1974); Mannes (1973); Russell (1975).

22. There are questions of validity, of course, relative to the two lay accounts. Both authors are reconstructing the dyings of their respective spouses largely from memory. However, for purposes of exploring the varying exigencies of control, the exact veracity of the accounts is not really of concern. A more serious problem arises from the obvious fact that none of these accounts was written with the questions and dimensions of present concern in mind.

23. It is interesting to compare Mrs. Abel's theory of pain medication administration with the almost identical theory of Cicely Saunders, founder of St. Christopher's Hospice (discussed below): "Eighty percent of the patients referred to the Hospice have pain sufficiently severe to need narcotics for its adequate relief. Many have had unrelieved pain for long periods and it may take time before they learn to expect relief rather than distress. Both are self-perpetuating, and the doctor should so anticipate the onset of pain that the patient does so no longer. Drugs balanced to need and given regularly so that pain does not occur prevent the vicious spiral of pain, tension, increased pain, and a higher dose of analgesic. The best treatment of terminal pain is its prevention" (Saunders, 1977: 171–172).

Part III

1. The activities here being scrutinized by no means exhaust the supply of collective enterprises that might fruitfully be viewed as coping with the modern face of death. Marshall (1976, 1975b), for example, has explored the organizational conditions for the development of death legitimations among residential groups of elderly. Hochschild's work (1973) is also relevant in this regard. So, too, the development of characteristic ideologies and practices among relevant

social locations—medical personnel, ministers, morticians, counsellors, etc.—might be similarly viewed as such "collective" enterprises. See, for example, Wood (1977, (1976b); Coombs and Powers (1976); Coombs and Goldman (1973); Charmaz (1976b); Glaser and Strauss (1965b, 1968); Warner (1959); Fulton (1961); Benoliel (1977); Garfield (1977); Habenstein and Lamers (1962); Unruh (1978); Turner and Edgley (1976). For purposes of this analysis, however, I shall restrict myself to those activities best conceived in social movement terms.

2. Other scholars and some participants, in referring to much the same phenomena, have begun to speak of the "natural death movement," the "death and dying movement," the "death with dignity movement," or the "death awareness movement." I prefer the sobriquet "happy death movement" because: (1) I believe it importantly captures, as we shall see, a crucial aspect of movement ideology; (2) because it is a more inclusive phrase than the alternatives; and (3) because I believe it provides the distancing necessary to speak *analytically* about something almost everyone else is speaking about *reverently*. I say, almost, because there are certainly some observers who view some of this activity with a thoroughly jaundiced eye. Let David Gutmann's comments stand as a prototype of this stance:

> Pop psychologists have reduced their production of books on achieving the good orgasm; instead they are now telling us how to compose an aesthetic decomposition—a graceful death. ... There are some obvious reasons for this lively interest in dying. In an age in which productive efforts have turned inward toward the cultivation of the perfect self, "hang-ups"—including the craven fear of death—are regarded as psychic blemishes, irrational curbs on personal freedom. Thus certain lumpen psychologists celebrate death, proclaiming this feat a proof of their inner liberation precisely because the unenlightened public fears to die. ... But the exhibitionism and provocativeness of trendy psychologists is not in itself sufficient to account for our recent cultural necrophilia. Like most symptoms, it is overdetermined—fed by many sources, some of them much more irrational than the necrophobia that they seek to undo. Thus, while taboo subjects are explored, the previously dehumanized members of society are at the same time rehumanized, sometimes even sentimentalized: blacks, women, homosexuals, the insane, and the aged. Along with these, the dying have entered the Third World, acquiring the kind of respectful awe that up to now was mainly reserved for successful murderers. Furthermore, as earnest theology students flock to their bedsides, the dying are treated to the kind

of intensive and often intrusive care which, if it does not hasten their demise, may at least make them welcome it. [Gutmann, 1977: 336; see also Langone, 1974: xvii; Hoppe, 1978]

3. As indicated, this "movement" is too diffuse for one to speak with great certainty about just *who* is in it. My observations here are based on knowledge about conference attendees, book authors and readership; some surveys of conference participants; the character of conference programs, symposia and workshops; organizational requisites for membership; and participation costs for a variety of activities.

4. Some recent conference titles provide a sense of the flavor and diversity of these events: "Death and Dying: Education, Counselling and Care"; "Achieving a Personal Death"; "Alternative Death Systems in America"; "The Art of Dying"; "The Child: Death Education and Counselling"; "Nursing Assessments and Approaches to the Care of the Terminally Ill Patient"; and "The 'How-to' of Hospice Care."

5. Fox and Crane (forthcoming) is a detailed analysis of what they call the "death and dying movement."

6. The scholarly literature expressing to a greater or lesser degree this "conventional perspective" is enormous. For an introduction, see Lindemann (1944); Kutscher, ed. (1969); Schoenberg et al., eds. (1975); Parkes (1972); Glick et al. (1974); Silverman (1976); Shneidman (1976); Clayton et al. (1976); Shoor and Speed (1976); Fulton and Fulton (1976). The popular literature is also huge and, in the late seventies, still growing. See, for example, Jackson (1957, 1962, 1971); Colgrove et al. (1976); Phipps (1974); Pincus (1974); Morris (1972); Osborne (1958); Kutscher and Kutscher (1971).

7. One of the odder developments in the emergence of death talk as a therapeutic specialty is Threshold, Inc., a Los Angeles-based organization that rents out dying companions. It is also interesting to note the tendency among those traditional comforters of the dying and grieving—the clergy—to utilize not a religious but a secular therapeutic paradigm in their current "death work." (See, for example, Wood, 1976b, 1977.)

8. See further, Farmer (1970); White (1970); Green and Irish, eds. (1971); Grollman, ed. (1967); Stein (1974).

9. The literature—both scholarly and popular-of this indictment is considerable. But see, for example, Glaser and Strauss (1965b, 1968); Coombs and Powers (1976); Crane (1975); Hinton (1967); Kübler-Ross (1969); Langone (1974); Maguire (I 974); Saunders (1977); Sudnow (1967); Mauksch (1975). If Snow's (1974) account of Chinese medical practice is at all accurate, it raises the possibility that bureaucratization of medical care is not in itself incompatible with the sort of dying care movement reformers advocate.

10. It is interesting to note that despite frequent reference in movement literature to Jessica Mitford's muckraking dissection of the American funeral industry (1963), little movement activity is devoted to reform in arrangements for the care of the *dead*. That is, there seems to be minimal attention to altering mortuary, funeral, or cemetary practices.

11. See further, Saunders (1959a, b, c, d, e, 1965, and 1977).

12. Among the more well known "successes" are Hospice, Inc. of New Haven; Palliative Care Service of Royal Victoria Hospital, Montreal and Hospice of Marin, California. On the New Haven Hospice, see Kron (1976).

13. MacDougall (1977) is relatively "pessimistic" as to the outcome, suggesting that Saunders-style changes "threaten the power of medical empires" (p. 12).

14. California's "natural death act" being one of the few successes.

15. See part I, note 22, for a sample of the relevant literature.

16. Manning (1970) is an early attempt to specify some of the difficulties and complexities of legalized "euthanasia." Bender (1974: ch. 2) provides a succinct review of the many issues involved in the debate.

17. See, for example, Back (1972); Fair (1974).

18. The extract from Kerr is from the written version (available for purchase from him) of the account of his son's death that he presented *orally* at a number of death and dying conferences and symposia.

See also on newspaper accounts of Kübler-Ross's "testimony": "Understanding Death: The Final Stage of Human Growth," *Sacramento Union* (May 27, 1975); "Psychiatrist sees afterlife," *Sacramento Bee* (September 20, 1975); "Expert on Death, the Dying, Is Not Turned Off on Life," *Sacramento Bee* (November 4, 1975). For additional accounts, see Gildea (1977); Balfour (1976); Woodward (1976); Hoover (1977a, 1977b); Panati (1976); Moody (1975); Kron (1976/1977); "Life after Death Experiences Cited," *Sacramento Union* (August 2, 1977).

Unquestionably, from the late sixties to the late seventies, Kübler-Ross served as a patron saint for important segments of the movement. She was "canonized" repeatedly at death and dying conferences—her name spoken in "hushed" and respectful tones. Some flavor of this sacred esteem is found in the following extract from a discussion of Kübler-Ross published in the *San Diego Reader* in 1978.

> Behind all the sociological terminology, behind the systematization of the stages of dying, behind the anecdotes and the moral advice [in her written work] there are the same age-old truths that in an earlier age were expressed by Saint Benedict or Guantama Buddha and by the institutions they helped to found.
>
> Dr. Kübler-Ross fits this role perfectly. Her modest demeanor, her quiet humor, her staunchness, her cheerfulness, her mixture of compassion and certainty, of gentleness and toughness, of delicate little body and tremendous moral strength: these are the characteristics of the nuns who work in hospitals, or among the extreme poor, or with the incurably ill. They are the recognizable characteristics of a certain kind of saint—in this case a thoroughly secular saint, let it be said. Dr. Kübler-Ross brings us the inescapable religious message, shorn of religion; and if *The Shadow Box* [a play about dying] does no more than make us turn to her writings and to her millennial wisdom, it will have served an invaluable function, whatever its artistic merits may be. [Saville, 1978]

19. I do not mean to suggest that this emerging ideological component has gone unchallenged. More traditional thanatology scholars have reacted with something less than enthusiasm. As Joan Kron, a senior editor for *New York* and a seasoned observer of the movement has written:

> Members of the thanatology community (who study death), however, had fits. After working for years to convince skeptics that the psychology of death and dying was a worthy subject for scientific study, one of their own members, Kübler-Ross (who was already getting flak from her colleagues for her

stages-of-dying theory), was now steering thanatology into spiritualist waters. "I admire Elisabeth tremendously," said one colleague, "but I don't believe in mixing one's religious beliefs with science." "I have left instructions," said another, "not to let that woman within a mile of my deathbed."

But most of the critical blasts are aimed at the 32-year-old Moody, a psychiatry resident, now on leave from the University of Virginia to write a sequel to his best-seller [*Life after Life*, 1975]. "As anecdotes, I'd give the book B-minus," says University of California professor of thanatology and suicide expert, Dr. Edwin Shneidman, "and as research, I'd give it D-minus." [Kron, 1976/1977: 71]

It is interesting to note also that Kübler-Ross has moved increasingly in the direction of mysticism. She does not report receiving messages from the deity, but she is hearing from spirits. (See, for example, Hoover, 1977a.) In the late seventies it remains unclear whether her exalted standing among movement participants will be sufficient for her to carry significant numbers of them with her into mysticism.

20. The seminar was sponsored by Reminding ("an organization that designs and coordinates seminars, workshops and conferences led by distinguished individuals in the humanities and sciences"), in cooperation with Dominican College, San Rafael, California and was held on the Dominican College campus, March 12–13, 1977 as part of the 1977 Dominican Series of Seminars. Dominican College was also the locale of a lecture by Dr. Cicely Saunders, on "The Philosophy of Hospice Care," sponsored by Hospice of Marin, August 26, 1977; and of a conference on "The How-to of Hospice Care" in May of that year.

21. One could also, of course, argue the obverse. The justification for my suggestion is primarily rhetorical rather than empirical.

22. The literature that might be viewed as supporting this assertion is considerable. See, for example, Hofstadter (1955); Rieff (1966); Halmos (1966); Schneider and Dornbusch (1958); Fair (1974); Meyer (1965); Back (1972); Sennott and Travisano (1976); Wolfe (1976); Noyes (1876); Treffert (1974).

Afterword

1. See, for example, Lauer and Handel (1977: 80–81); Lindesmith et al. (1975); Secord et al. (1976: 270); Secord and Backman (1974: 413–419); Turner (1968: 552–556).

2. One of the reasons, perhaps, that caricature of, and satire on, modern identities is a flourishing trade. Cyra McFadden's *The Serial: A Year in the Life of Marin County* (1977) is a deservedly successful example.

3. For an insightful discussion of the "ups and downs" of public attention to issues, see Downs (1972).

4. Cottle (1975), provides a nice critique of the contemporary American penchant for "soul-baring."

5. Keyes (1975) suggests some of the negative consequences of self-improvement as an American growth industry.

Bibliography

Alsop, Stewart (1973) *Stay of Execution: A Sort of Memoir.* J. P. Lippincott.

Anonymous (1975) "Donald Malcolm." *The New Yorker* September 8: 128.

—— (1968) "Variations in mortality from influenza and pneumonia by socioeconomic level." *Statistical Bulletin,* Metropolitan Life Insurance January: 5–7.

—— (1957) "A way of dying." *Atlantic Monthly* January: 53–55.

Aries, Philippe (1974a) "The reversal of death: changes in attitudes toward death in Western societies," in David E. Stannard (ed.), *Death in America.* University of Pennsylvania Press, pp. 134–158.

—— (1974b) *Western Attitudes toward Death from the Middle Ages to the Present.* Johns Hopkins University Press.

—— (1962) *Centuries of Childhood.* Alfred A. Knopf.

Aubert, Vilhelm, and Harrison White (1968) "Sleep: a sociological interpretation," in Marcello Truzzi (ed.), *Sociology and Everyday Life.* Prentice-Hall, pp. 325–345.

Back, Kurt W. (1972) *Beyond Words: The Story of Sensitivity Training and the Encounter Movement.* Russell Sage Foundation.

Balfour, Malcolm (1976) "Trappist monk describes his ecstatic experience of life after death." *National Enquirer* November 19.

Barbellion, W. N. P. (1920) A *Last Diary*. Chatto and Windus (London).

—— (1919) *The Journal of a Disappointed Man*. Chatto and Windus (London).

Barber, Theodore X. (1961) "Death by suggestion." *Psychosomatic Medicine* 23, 2: 153–155.

Basayne, Hank (1974) "Ars Moriendi: The Art of Dying." Brochure for Association for Humanistic Psychology sponsored conference on "The Art of Dying."

Behnke, John A. and Sissela Bok [eds.] (1975) *The Dilemmas of Euthanasia*. Doubleday Anchor.

Bender, David L. [ed.] (1974) *Problems of Death: Opposing Viewpoints*. Greenhaven Press.

Benedict, Ruth (1934) *Patterns of Culture*. New American Library (Mentor edition, 1946).

Benoliel, Jeanne Quint (1977) "Nurses and the human experience of dying," in Herman Feifel (ed.), *New Meanings of Death*. McGraw-Hill. pp. 123–142.

Berger, Peter L. and Thomas Luckmann (1967) *The Social Construction of Reality*. Doubleday Anchor.

Bernstein, Burton (1975) *Thurber: A Biography*. Dodd, Mead.

Blauner, Robert (1966) "Death and social structure." *Psychiatry* 24: 378–394.

Blumer, Herbert (1971) "Social problems as collective behavior." *Social Problems* Winter: 298–306.

—— (1969a) "Social movements," in Barry McLaughlin (ed.), *Studies in Social Movements: A Social Psychological Perspective*. The Free Press. pp. 8–20.

—— (1969b) "Collective behavior," in Alfred McClung Lee (ed.) *Principles of Sociology*, 3rd ed., Barnes and Noble, pp. 65–120.

Bottel, Helen (1976) "Helen help us." *Sacramento Bee* July 30.

Bowra, Maurice, et al. (1952) *Golden Ages of the Great Cities.* Thames and Hudson.

Byrne, M. St. Clare (1961) *Elizabethan Life in Town and Country.* Barnes and Noble (first published, 1925).

Cannon, Walter (1942) "Voodoo death." *American Anthropologist* April/ June: 169–181.

Capron, Alexander Morgan, and Leon R. Kass (1972–73) "A statutory definition of the standards for determining human death: an appraisal and a proposal." *University of Pennsylvania Law Review* 121:87–118.

Carcopino, Jerome (1940) *Daily Life in Ancient Rome: The People and the City at the Height of the Empire.* Yale University Press.

Charmaz, Kathy Calkins (in press) *The Social Reality of Death.* Addison-Wesley.

—— (1977) "Time perspectives of the chronically ill." Paper presented at the meetings of the American Sociological Association, Chicago, September.

—— (1976a) "A symbolic interactionist critique of Kübler-Ross's stages of dying." Paper presented at the meetings of the American Sociological Association, New York, August–September.

—— (1976b) "The coroner's strategies for announcing death," in Lyn H. Lofland (ed.), *Toward a Sociology of Death and Dying.* Sage, pp. 61–81.

Childe, V. Gordon (1942) *What Happened in History.* Penguin Books.

Clayton, Paula, Lynn Desmarais and George Winokur (1976) "A study of normal bereavement," in Robert Fulton (ed.), *Death and Identity.* The Charles Press, pp. 222–239.

Cohn, Al (1975) "Who takes over? Dying mom crusades for homemaker insurance." *Sacramento Bee* August 17.

122   **Bibliography**

Colgrove, Melba, Harold H. Bloomfield and Peter McWilliams (1976) *How to Survive the Loss of a Love: 58 Things to Do When There Is Nothing to Be Done*. Lion Press.

Comper, Frances M. M. [ed.] (1917) *The Book of the Craft of Dying and Other Early English Tracts Concerning Death*. Longmans, Green, and Co.

Coombs, Robert H., and Pauline S. Powers (1976) "Socialization for death: the physician's role," in Lyn H. Lofland (ed), *Toward a Sociology of Death and Dying*. Sage, pp. 15–36.

Coombs, Robert H., and L. J. Goldman (1973) "Maintenance and discontinuity of coping mechanisms in an intensive-care unit." *Social Problems* Winter: 342–355.

Cottle, Thomas J. (1975) "Our soul-baring orgy destroys the private self," *Psychology Today* October: 22–23 and 87.

Crane, Diana (1975) *The Sanctity of Social life: Physicians' Treatment of Critically Ill Patients*. Russell Sage Foundation.

Cutter, Fred (1974) *Coming to Terms with Death*. Nelson-Hall.

Demuth, Bob (1973) "Cancer victim says she's lucky." *The Davis Enterprise* May 30.

Dingle, John H. (1973) "The ills of man." *Scientific American* September: 77–84.

Donaldson, Peter J. (1972) "Denying death: a note regarding some ambiguities in the current discussion." *Omega* November: 285–290.

Douce, Francis (1833) *The Dance of Death*. William Pickering.

Downing, A. B. [ed.] (1969) *Euthanasia and the Right to Death: The Case for Voluntary Euthanasia*. Peter Owen.

Downs, Anthony (1972) "Up and down with ecology—the 'Issue-Attention Cycle.' " *The Public Interest* Summer: 38–50.

Dumont, Richard G. and Dennis C. Foss (1972) *The American View of Death: Acceptance or Denial?* Schenkman.

Durant, Celeste (1976) "Nancy—spell it indomitable." *The Los Angeles Times* May 28.

Fair, Charles (1974) *The New Nonsense.* Simon and Schuster.

Farmer, James A., Jr. (1970) "Death education: adult education in the face of a taboo." *Omega* May: 109–113.

Fox, Renée C. (1959) *Experiment Perilous.* The Free Press.

Fox, Renée C., and Diana Crane (forthcoming) *The Death and Dying Movement.*

Fulton, Robert (1961) "The clergyman and the funeral director: a study in role conflict." *Social Forces* 39: 317–323.

Fulton, Robert, and Julie Fulton (1976) "A psychosocial aspect of terminal care: anticipatory grief," in Robert Fulton (ed.), *Death and Identity.* The Charles Press, pp. 323–335.

Garfield, Charles A. (1977) "Impact of death on the health-care professional," in Herman Feifel (ed.), *New Meanings of Death.* McGraw-Hill, pp. 143–151.

George, M. Dorothy (1965) *London Life in the 18th Century.* Capricorn Books.

Gerlach, Luther P., and Virginia H. Hine (1970) *People, Power and Change: Movements of Social Transformation.* Bobbs-Merrill.

Gildea, William (1977) "Life ... after death." *Sacramento Bee* June 27.

Glaser, Barney, and Anselm Strauss (1971) *Status Passage.* Aldine-Atherton.

—— (1968) *Time for Dying.* Aldine.

—— (1965a) "Temporal aspects of dying as a non-scheduled status passage." *American Journal of Sociology* July: 48–59.

—— (1965b) *Awareness of Dying.* Aldine.

Glick, Ira O., Robert S. Weiss and C. Murray Parkes (1974) *The First Year of Bereavement.* Wiley-Interscience.

Glock, Charles, and Rodney Stark (1965) *Religion and Society in Tension.* Rand McNally.

Goffman, Erving (1963) *Stigma.* Prentice-Hall.

Goldscheider, Calvin (1976) "The mortality revolution," in Edwin S. Shneidman (ed.), *Death: Current Perspectives.* Mayfield Publishing, pp. 163–189.

—— (1971) *Population, Modernization and Social Structure.* Little, Brown.

Goode, William J. (1970) *World Revolution and Family Patterns.* Free Press Paperback.

Gordon, David Cole (1970) *Overcoming the Fear of Death.* Macmillan.

Gove, Walter R. (1973) "Sex, marital status and mortality." *American Journal of Sociology* July: 45–67.

Gowen, B. S. (1907) "Some aspects of pestilences and other epidemics." *American Journal of Psychology* January: 1–60.

Green, Betty R., and Donald P. Irish [eds.] (1971) *Death Education: Preparation for Living.* Schenkman.

Greenfield, Natalee S. (1976) *First Do No Harm.* Two Continents.

Grollman, Earl A. (1970) *Talking about Death: A Dialogue between Parent and Child.* Beacon Press.

—— [ed.] (1967) *Explaining Death to Children.* Beacon Press.

Gubrium, Jaber F. (1976) "Death worlds in a nursing home," in Lyn H. Lofland (ed.), *Toward a Sociology of Death and Dying.* Sage, pp. 83–104.

—— (1975) *Living and Dying at Murray Manor.* St. Martin's Press.

Gustafson, Elizabeth (l 972) "Dying: the career of the nursing home patient." *Journal of Health and Social Behavior* September: 226–235.

Gutmann, David (1977) "Dying to power: death and the search for self-esteem," in Herman Feifel (ed.), *New Meanings of Death.* McGraw-Hill, pp. 335–347.

Habenstein, Robert W., and William M. Lamers (1962) *The History of American Funeral Directing*. Bulfin Printers.

Halmos, Paul (1966) *The Faith of the Counsellors*. Schocken.

Hendin, David (1973) *Death as a Fact of Life*. W. W. Norton.

Hertz, Robert (1960) *Death and the Right Hand*. Free Press.

Hicks, David (1975) "A slow and orderly dying." *Human Behavior* March: 17–22.

Hillery, George A., Jr., et al. (1968) "Causes of death in the demographic transition." Paper presented at the annual meeting of the Population Association of America. Boston, April.

Hinton, John (1967) *Dying*. Penguin Books.

Hochschild, A. R. (1973) *The Unexpected Community*. Prentice-Hall.

Hofstadter, Richard (1955) *The Age of Reform*. Vintage Books.

Holmes, Urban Tigner, Jr. (1966) *Daily Living in the Twelfth Century*. University of Wisconsin Press.

Honig, Ana (1975) "The last victim of smallpox," *San Francisco Sunday Examiner and Chronicle* August 31.

Hoover, Eleanor Links (1977a) "Mystical portents." *Human Behavior* March: 14.

—— (1977b) "Charting life after death." *Human Behavior* April: 9.

Hoppe, Art (1978) "A dying fad." *San Francisco Chronicle* April 30.

Howard, Alan, and Robert A. Scott (1965–66) "Cultural values and attitudes toward death." *Journal of Existentialism* 6: 161–174.

Huizinga, J. (1963) *The Waning of the Middle Ages*. Doubleday Anchor.

Hunter, R. C. (1967) "On the experience of nearly dying." *American Journal of Psychiatry* July: 84–88.

Imara, Mwalimu (1975) "Dying as the last stage of growth," in Elisabeth Kübler-Ross (ed.), *Death: The Final Stage of Growth*. Prentice-Hall, pp. 147–163.

Jackson, Edgar (1971) *When Someone Dies*. Fortress.

—— (1962) *You and Your Grief*. Hawthorn.

—— (1957) *Understanding Grief: Its Roots, Dynamics and Treatment*. Abingdon.

Kalish, Richard A. (1970) "The onset of the dying process." *Omega* February: 57–69.

Kastenbaum, Robert (1977) "Introduction" in the First Announcement of the Arno Press Reprint Series on "The Literature of Death and Dying."

Kastenbaum, Robert and Ruth Aisenberg (1972) *The Psychology of Death*. Springer.

Kavanaugh, Robert E. (1972) *Facing Death*. Penguin.

Keleman, Stanley (1974) *Living Your Dying*. Random House.

Kerr, Keith W. (1974) "Death and grief counselling," mimeographed. Presented in part at "Alternative Death Systems in America" Conference, University of California, Berkeley, February 21–23, 1975. Earlier version published in *The Marriage and Family Counselors Quarterly* Winter, 1972.

Keyes, Ralph (1975) "I'm OK, you're probably OK." *Newsweek* October 13: 20.

Klein, Norma (1976) *Sunshine*. Holt, Rinehart and Winston.

Koestenbaum, Peter (1976) *Is There an Answer to Death?* Prentice-Hall.

Kohl, Marvin (1974) *The Morality of Killing*. Humanities Press.

Kron, Joan (1976/77) "The out-of-body trip: what a way to go!" *New York,* December 27/January 3: 66–72.

—— (1976) "Designing a better place to die." *New York* March 1: 43–49.

—— (1975) "The good news about the bad news." *New York* July 21: 38–40.

—— (1973) "Learning to live with death." *Philadelphia Magazine* April.

Kübler-Ross, Elisabeth [ed.] (1975) *Death: The Final Stage of Growth.* Prentice-Hall.

—— (1969) *On Death and Dying.* Macmillan.

Kutscher, Austin H. [ed.] (1969) *Death and Bereavement.* Charles C. Thomas.

Kutscher, Austin H., and Lillian G. Kutscher [eds.] (1971) *For the Bereaved.* Frederick Fell.

Lacroix, Paul (1963) *France in the Middle Ages,* Frederick Ungar. First published as *Manners, Customs and Dress during the Middle Ages and during the Renaissance Period* (1876).

Langone, John (1974) *Vital Signs.* Little, Brown.

Laurence, John (1960) *A History of Capital Punishment.* Citadel.

Lauer, Robert H., and Warren H. Handel (1977) *Social Psychology: The Theory and Application of Symbolic Interactionism.* Houghton Mifflin.

Lenski, Gerhard (1970) *Human Societies: A Macrolevel Introduction to Sociology.* McGraw-Hill.

Lerner, Monroe (1970) "When, why, and where people die." in Orville Brim, Jr. et al. (eds.) *The Dying Patient.* Russell Sage Foundation, pp. 5–29.

Levy, Robert I. (1973) *Tahitians: Mind and Experience in the Society Islands.* University of Chicago Press.

Lindemann, Erich (1944) "Symptomatology and management of acute grief." *American Journal of Psychiatry* September: 141–148.

Lindesmith, Alfred R., Anselm L. Strauss and Norman K. Denzin (1975) *Social Psychology.* Dryden Press.

Lofland, John (1977) "The dramaturgy of state executions," in Horace Bleackley and John Lofland, *State Executions Viewed Historically and Sociologically*. Patterson Smith, pp. 275–325.

—— (1976a) *Doing Social Life: The Qualitative Study of Human Interaction in Natural Settings*. Wiley-Interscience.

—— (1976b) "Open and Concealed Dramaturgic Strategies: The Case of the State Execution," in Lyn H. Lofland (ed.), *Toward a Sociology of Death and Dying*. Sage, pp. 37–60.

—— (1969) *Deviance and Identity* (with the assistance of Lyn H. Lofland). Prentice-Hall.

Lofland, Lyn H. (1976) "Toward a sociology of death and dying: editor's introduction," in Lyn H. Lofland (ed.), *Toward a Sociology of Death and Dying*. Sage, pp. 7–13.

Lopata, Helena Znaniecki (1973) *Widowhood in an American City*. Schenkman.

Lottman, Herbert T. (1975) "Paris: the novel salon." The Guest Word, *New York Times Book Review* November 16: 87.

MacDougall; John (1977) "Professionals, power and new ways of dying." Unpublished paper.

Macleod, Scott (1975) "Family treats death with terminal candor." *The Sacramento Union* September 8.

Maguire, Daniel (1974) *Death By Choice*. Schocken.

Malinowski, Bronislaw (1954) *Magic, Science and Religion*. Doubleday Anchor.

Mannes, Marya (1973) *Last Rights: A Case for the Good Death*. New American Library.

Manning, Bayless (1970) "Legal and policy issues in the allocation of death," in Orville Brim, Jr. et al. (eds.), *The Dying Patient*, Russell Sage Foundation, pp. 253–274.

Mant, A. Keith (1976) "The medical definition of death," in Edwin S. Shneidman (ed.), *Death: Current Perspectives.* Mayfield, pp. 218–231.

Marcuse, Herbert (1959) "The ideology of death," in Herman Feifel (ed.), *The Meaning of Death.* McGraw-Hill, pp. 64–76.

Marshall, Victor W. (1976) "Organizational features of terminal status passage in residential facilities for the aged," in Lyn H. Lofland (ed.), *Toward a Sociology of Death and Dying,* Sage, pp. 115–134.

—— (1975a) "Fear, denial and legitimation of death." Unpublished paper.

—— (1975b) "Socialization for impending death in a retirement village." *American Journal of Sociology* March: 1124–1144.

—— (1975c) "No exit: aging as a terminal status passage." Paper presented at the 28th Annual Meeting, Gerontological Society, Louisville, Kentucky, October.

Mauksch, Hans O. (1975) "The organizational context of dying," in Elisabeth Kübler-Ross (ed.), *Death: The Final Stage of Growth.* Prentice-Hall, pp. 7–24.

Mayhew, Henry (1950) *London's Underworld,* edited by Peter Quennell. Selections from "Those That Will Not Work," Vol. 4 of *London Labor and the London Poor,* first published 1862.

McCoy, Marjorie C. (1974) *To Die with Style!* Abingdon Press.

McFadden, Cyra (1977) *The Serial: A Year in the Life of Marin County.* Alfred A. Knopf.

McNeill, William H. (1976) *Plagues and Peoples.* Doubleday Anchor.

Meyer, Donald (1965) *The Positive Thinkers.* Doubleday.

Miller, John C. (1966) *The First Frontier: Life in Colonial America.* Dell.

Mitford, Jessica (1963) *The American Way of Death.* Fawcett.

Moody, Raymond A. (1975) *Life after Life.* Mockingbird Books.

Moore, Wilbert E., and Melvin M. Tumin (1949) "Some social functions of ignorance." *American Sociological Review* December: 787–795.

Morison, Robert S. (1973) "Dying." *Scientific American* September: 55–62.

Morris, Sarah (1972) *Grief and How to Live with It*. The Family Inspiration Library.

Nichols, Roy and Jane Nichols (1975) "Funerals: a time for grief and growth," in Elisabeth Kübler-Ross (ed.), *Death: The Final Stage of Growth*. Prentice-Hall, pp. 87–96.

Nohl, J. (1961) *The Black Death*. Ballantine.

Noyes, John Humphrey (1876) *Mutual Criticism*. Office of the American Socialist in Oneida.

Noyes, Russell, Jr., and Roy Kletti (1972) "The experience of dying from falls." *Omega* February: 45–52.

O'Connor, Sister Mary Catharine (1942) *The Art of Dying Well: The Development of the Ars Moriendi*. Columbia University Press.

Osborne, Ernest (1958) *When You Lose a Loved One*. Public Affairs Pamphlet No. 269, Public Affairs Committee.

Panati, Charles (1976) "Is there life after death." *Family Circle* November: 78, 84 and 90.

Parkes, Colin Murray (1972) *Bereavement: Studies of Grief in Adult Life*. International Universities Press.

—— (1964) "Effects of bereavement on physical and mental health: a study of the medical records of widows." *British Medical Journal* pp. 274–279.

Parsons, Talcott, Renée C. Fox and Victor M. Lidz (1973) "The 'gift of life' and its reciprocation," in Arien Mack (ed.), *Death in American Experience*. Schocken, pp. 1–49.

Parsons, Talcott, and Victor Lidz (1967) "Death in American society," in Edwin S. Shneidman (ed.), *Essays in Self-Destruction*. Science House, pp. 133–170.

Pattison, E. M. (1967) "The experience of dying." *American Journal of Psychotherapy* January: 32–43.

Phipps, Joyce (1974) *Death's Single Privacy: Grieving and Personal Growth.* The Seabury Press.

Pincus, Lily (1974) *Death and the Family: The Importance of Mourning.* Vintage Books.

Preston, Samuel H., Nathan Keyfitz and Robert Schoen (1972) *Causes of Death: Life Tables for National Populations.* Seminar Press.

Richter, Curt P. (1959) "The phenomenon of unexplained sudden death in animals and man," in Herman Feifel (ed.), *The Meaning of Death.* McGraw-Hill, pp. 302–313.

Rieff, Philip (1966) *The Triumph of the Therapeutic.* Harper and Row.

Rosenthal, Ted (1973) *How Could I Not Be among You.* George Braziller.

Rothenberg, Albert (1961) "Psychological problems in terminal cancer management. *Cancer* September/October: 1063–1073.

Rowling, Marjorie (1968) *Everyday Life in Medieval Times.* G. P. Putnam's Sons.

Russell, O. Ruth (1975) *Freedom to Die: Moral and Legal Aspects of Euthanasia.* Dell Publishing.

Saunders, Cicely (1977) "Dying they live: St. Christopher's Hospice," in Herman Feifel, *New Meanings of Death.* McGraw-Hill, pp. 154–179.

—— (1969) "The moment of truth: care of the dying person," in Leonard Pearson (ed.), *Death and Dying: Current Issues in the Treatment of the Dying Person.* The Press of Case Western Reserve University, pp. 49–78.

—— (1965) "The last stages of life." *American Journal of Nursing* March: 70–75.

—— (1959a) "The problem of euthanasia." *Nursing Times* October 9: 960–961.

—— (1959b) "Should a patient know ... ? *Nursing Times* October 16: 994–995.

—— (1959c) "Mental distress in the dying," *Nursing Times* October 30: 1067–1069.

—— (1959d) "The nursing of patients dying of cancer." *Nursing Times* November 6: 1091–1092.

—— (1959e) "When a patient is dying." *Nursing Times* November 13: 1129–1130.

Saville, Jonathan (1978) "Death mask." *San Diego Reader* April 13–19.

Schneider, L., and S. Dornbusch (1958) *Popular Religion: Inspirational Books in America:* University of Chicago Press.

Schulz, Richard and David Aderman (1974) "Clinical research and the stages of dying." *Omega* Summer: 137–143.

Schoenberg, Bernard, et al. [eds.] (1975) *Bereavement: Its Psychosocial Aspects.* Columbia University Press.

Secord, Paul F., and Carl W. Backman (1974) *Social Psychology.* McGraw-Hill.

Secord, Paul F., Carl W. Backman and David R. Slavitt (1976) *Understanding Social Life: An Introduction to Social Psychology.* McGraw-Hill.

Seligman, Jean (with Susan Agrest) (1977) "A death in the family." *Newsweek* June 20: 89.

Sennott, Roger S., and Richard V. Travisano (1976) "Puritanism and rationality: the socially impossible consciousness." Paper presented at the meetings of the Society for the Study of Symbolic Interaction, New York, August 31.

Sheskin, Arlene (in press) *Why Die? Extend Your Life Through Cryonics: A Study of Belief Systems and Bereavement.* Irvington Publishers, Inc.

Shibles, Warren (1974) *Death: An Interdisciplinary Analysis.* The Language Press.

Shneidman, Edwin S. (1976) "Death work and stages of dying," in Edwin S. Shneidman (ed.), *Death: Current Perspectives*. Mayfield Publishing, pp. 443–451.

Shoor, Mervyn, and Mary H. Speed (1976) "Death, delinquency and the mourning process," in Robert Fulton (ed.), *Death and Identity*. The Charles Press, pp. 258–263.

Silver, Allan (1967) "On the demand for order in civil society: a review of some themes in the history of urban crime, police and riot," in David J. Bordua (ed.), *The Police*. John Wiley and Sons, pp. 1–24.

Silverman, Phyllis Rolfe (1976) "The widow-to-widow program: an experiment in preventive intervention," in Edwin S. Shneidman (ed.), *Death: Current Perspectives*. Mayfield Publishing, pp. 356–363.

Simmons, Leo W. (1945) *The Role of the Aged in Primitive Society*. Yale University Press.

Sjoberg, Gideon (1960) *The Preindustrial City*. The Free Press.

Snell, David (1967) "How it feels to die." *Life*, May 26.

Snow, Lois Wheeler (1974) *Death with Dignity: When the Chinese Came*, Random House.

Spiegel, John (1964) "Cultural variations in attitudes toward death and disease," in G. Grosse et al. (eds.), *The Threat of Impending Disaster*. MIT Press, 283–299.

Stair, John Bettridge (1897) *Old Samoa: Or, Flotsam and Jetsam From the Pacific Ocean*. The Religious Tract Society (Human Relations Area Files, Microfiche OU8, Card 065, Category 763).

Stannard, David E. (1973) "Death and dying in Puritan New England." *American Historical Review* December: 1305–1330.

Stein, Sara Bonnett (1974) *About Dying: An Open Family Book for Parents and Children Together*. Walker.

Strauss, Anselm L., and Barney G. Glaser (1970) *Anguish*. Sociology Press.

Sudnow, David (1967) *Passing On: The Social Organization of Dying.* Prentice-Hall.

Treffert, Darold A. (1974) "Why Amy didn't live happily ever after." *Prism* November.

Turner, Ralph (1968) "Role: sociological aspects." *International Encyclopedia of the Social Sciences,* Vols. 13 and 14. Macmillan and The Free Press, pp. 552–556.

—— (1962) "Role taking: process versus conformity," in Arnold M. Rose (ed.), *Human Behavior and Social Processes.* Houghton Mifflin, pp. 20–40.

Turner, Ralph H., and Lewis M. Killian (1972) *Collective Behavior.* Prentice-Hall.

Turner, Ronny E., and Charles Edgley (1976) "Death as theater: a dramaturgical analysis of the American funeral." *Sociology and Social Research* July: 378–392.

Unruh, David (1978) "Doing funeral directing: managing sources of risk in funeralization." Unpublished manuscript.

Veatch, Robert M. (1976a) "Brain death," in Edwin S. Shneidman (ed.), *Death: Current Perspectives.* Mayfield, pp. 232–240.

—— (1976b) *Death, Dying and the Biological Revolution: Our Last Quest for Responsibility.* Yale University Press.

Vernon, Glenn M. (1970) *Sociology of Death: An Analysis of Death Related Behavior.* Ronald Press.

Vernon, Glenn M., and Charles E. Waddell (1974) "Dying as social behavior: Mormon behavior through half a century." *Omega* Fall: 199–206.

Walter, Mary Jane (1944) "Psychic death: report of a possible case." *Archives of Neurology and Psychiatry* 52: 84–85.

Warner, W. Lloyd (1959) *The Living and the Dead: A Study of the Symbolic Life of Americans.* Yale University Press.

Weisman, Avery (1973) "Coping with untimely death." *Psychiatry* November: 366–378.

Weisman, Avery D., and T. P. Hackett, (1976) "Predilection to death," in Robert Fulton (ed.), *Death and Identity.* The Charles Press, pp. 288–317.

Wertenbaker, Lael (1957) *Death of a Man.* Random House.

White, Douglas K. (1970) "An undergraduate course in death." *Omega* August: 167–174.

Williams, Robert H. [ed.] (1973) *To Live and to Die: When, Why and How.* Springer-Verlag, pp. 134–149.

Wilson, Bryan P. (1966) *Religion in Secular Society.* C. A. Watts.

Wilson, John (1973) *Introduction to Social Movements.* Basic Books.

Winter, A. [ed.] (1969) *The Moment of Death: A Symposium.* Charles C. Thomas.

Wolfe, Tom (1976) "The me decade and the third great awakening." *New West* August 30: 27–48.

Wood, Juanita (1977) "Expressive death: the current death work paradigm." Ph.D. dissertation, University of California, Davis, unpublished.

—— (1976a) "Death as a 'NOW' issue." Paper presented at the annual meetings of the American Sociological Association, New York, September.

—— (1976b) "The structure of concern: the ministry in death-related situations," in Lyn H. Lofland (ed.), *Toward a Sociology of Death and Dying.* Sage, pp. 135–150.

—— (1972) "A working paper on being terminally ill." University of California, Davis, unpublished manuscript.

Woodward, Kenneth L. (1976) "Life after death." *Newsweek* July 12: 41.

Wrigley, E. A. (1969) *Population and History.* McGraw-Hill.

Yawger, N. S. (1936) "Emotions as the cause of rapid and sudden death." *Archives of Neurology and Psychiatry* 36: 875–879.

About the Author

Lyn H. Lofland is a Professor Emerita in the Department of Sociology at the University of California, Davis. Her publications—reflecting her interest in social interaction and psychology, community and urban sociology, qualitative methodologies, and the sociology of death and dying—include *A World of Strangers: Order and Action in Urban Public Space, Analyzing Social Settings: A Guide to Qualitative Observation and Analysis* (with John Lofland, David Snow, and Leon Anderson), and the edited volume *Toward a Sociology of Death and Dying.*